Economic Principles for Prosperity

by Robert P. Murphy, Jason Clemens,
Milagros Palacios, and Niels Veldhuis

Fraser Institute
www.fraserinstitute.org
2014

Date of issue: 2014
Printed and bound in Canada

Cover design and artwork
Monica Thomas, Foothills Graphics

Library and Archives Canada Cataloguing in Publication Data

Economic Principles for Prosperity / Robert P. Murphy, Jason Clemens, Milagros Palacios, and Niels Veldhuis

Includes bibliographical references.
ISBN 978-0-88975-304-4.

Contents

Contents, continued

III Economic myths and how they prevent progress

Economic Principles for Prosperity

Introduction

A central goal of the Fraser Institute is to provide interested Canadians with information about what works and what doesn't when it comes to creating, maintaining, and improving prosperity.

Often when people talk of prosperity, they conceptualize it in very narrow terms. For them, prosperity simply means money. Having money is no doubt a critical aspect of prosperity, but it is just that—one aspect. Other aspects of prosperity include a robust job market where employment is available and opportunities for advancement abound, an employment environment where upward mobility is based on hard work and on the acquisition of formal and informal education and training, and where invention is encouraged. In a prosperous economy, individuals are able to innovate, creating new and better products, services, and ways of doing things.

A prosperous society also extends far beyond the working world. It includes an aspirational education system where children are taught not only the basics and critical thinking, but given the tools and confidence to aspire and dream. It includes a health care system that responds to the needs of the sick but also acts to prevent illness so as to achieve a healthy and productive society. It includes a clean and sustainable environment. It includes and encourages empathy by its citizens to care for the less fortunate and those in need using the most effective means available.

In short, our view of a prosperous society is one that affords opportunities to everyone for personal and professional fulfilment. This book is about how best to achieve those aims. One of the book's underlying tenets is that stagnation has been the overwhelming norm for human society. We recognize that the remarkable progress that began to take hold in the 18th century is atypical in the scope of human history.

This book is divided into three distinct but related parts. The first section gives readers ten basic economic principles that we believe are essential for economic prosperity. Better understanding these principles can lead to a better understanding of the general principles that should guide government policy. They include many simple concepts such as "incentives matter" and "workers can only consume more if they first produce more." And yet we are constantly amazed at the number of times these basic principles are misunderstood, ignored, or simply unknown.

The book's second section describes seven key institutions that are prerequisites for societies to advance and progress. They are not, in and of themselves, sufficient to ensure prosperity, but we are unaware of any society that has prospered without these core institutions. "Institutions" is a fairly vague description of what are concrete rules, incentives, and laws that create the environment within which individuals and groups of people act within a society. We provide a description of these institutions—including an unbiased, functioning legal system, sound money, and the ability to trade with others—along with evidence as to how they contribute to a fruitful environment within which economic progress can flourish. These institutions are largely but not exclusively based on the path-breaking work of the Fraser Institute's Economic Freedom of the World initiative.

Finally, section three of this book discusses fifteen prominent myths and commonly held misperceptions that often impede improvement. The first and perhaps most prominent myth has hindered real reform in Canada's health care system for the better part of two decades: namely, that any change to the country's health care system will inevitably lead to an American system of health care. This is, on its face, an absurdity; there are a number of developed countries—Australia, France, Japan, Germany, the Netherlands, Sweden, and Switzerland—that offer universal health care, but do so in dramatically different ways from Canada. Other myths related to education, taxation, charitable giving, and the environment are all empirically explored and discussed. This last section aims to give readers greater clarity about many pressing issues facing Canada, some of which could be resolved were many of our fellow citizens not wedded to the myths discussed.

By teaching economic principles, explaining the institutional prerequisites for prosperity, and shattering economic myths, this book equips everyone with the intellectual tools we need to achieve a more prosperous Canada.

Robert P. Murphy, Jason Clemens, Milagros Palacios, and Niels Veldhuis

CHAPTER ONE

Economic principles

Think like an economist

Before we can explore what economists have to say about institutions (the focus of Chapter Two) or debunk common myths in policy discussions (the focus of Chapter Three), we first need to develop the economist's toolkit. That is, we need to understand some of the key principles (or what some might call economic "laws") that economists bring to the table when they enter a discussion. In short, we must learn to "think like an economist."

The ten economic principles laid out in this chapter constitute a particular *way of viewing the world*. They give us a lens or filter through which the economist interprets not just narrowly construed "economic" matters—such as jobs, gross domestic product (GDP), and prices—but the very institutions underpinning society itself. As we will see, these ten principles should strike most readers as intuitive, just by reading them and thinking through their meaning.

Yet even though the following principles will seem straightforward and obvious at first, their *implications* are not obvious. Indeed, the purpose of this book is to educate the public on the findings of economics, concerning very important matters affecting the prosperity of the home, the nation, and even the entire world. In the second and third chapters, we will see how these apparently simple principles can lead to startling conclusions, which fly in the face of what "everyone knows" about private enterprise and government policy.

Economic Principle #1

Incentives matter

The most succinct expression of the economic way of thinking comes down to a simple, two-word sentence: "Incentives matter." This principle relies on the fact that people have goals that they are trying to achieve, and that they will therefore act differently, depending on the circumstances. An incentive is simply anything that induces action or motivates effort. In other words, they are the costs and benefits you pay or receive from a particular decision.

Physicists don't need to worry about incentives in their field of study. After all, the cannonball's trajectory through the air has nothing to do with where it "wants" to go; it is determined by the laws of physics. But in economics, we must always keep in mind that the objects of our study are thinking individuals who have their own purposes, and that they may suddenly *change their behaviour* in response to a new environment.

There are cases where it's obvious that incentives matter. For example, parents may threaten to ground their teenager for particular transgressions—a disincentive—or promise access to the family car if high grades are earned—an incentive. The parents do this—obviously—because they want to *influence their child's behaviour*. Continuing with the example, it is common advice for new parents that if they are going to threaten a punishment, then they had better follow through with it, lest the child learns to ignore their warnings in the future. In short, incentives matter.

Another obvious example, more relevant to economic issues, is that workers respond to wages. In a private enterprise system, where economic activity undertaken by individuals and/or organizations that have ownership over resources such as capital and labour, an expanding industry attracts new workers with the promise of higher wages (and better working conditions). It is important for people to have the proper *incentives* to behave productively. To see why, imagine a college professor announced in the beginning of the semester that everyone in the class would receive the "average" score of the final exam, rather than each student getting the grade that he or she actually earned on the exam. With such incentives in place, what would happen to the amount of studying that the class put in?

I quit. They're too expensive.

Although everyone can recognize that incentives matter in certain contexts, it is surprising how often non-economists fail to apply the principle consistently. For example, most Canadians recognize that a special tax placed on tobacco will, in addition to raising revenue, tend to discourage people from smoking. By the same token, environmentalists concerned about climate change applaud British Columbia's carbon tax, since it will discourage carbon dioxide emissions from the province. Yet when economists warn that the relatively onerous federal- and provincial-income tax burden will discourage income growth in Canada, many Canadians dismiss the warnings as nonsense. For some reason, these people recognize that tax incentives matter when it comes to smoking and carbon emissions, but they think tax incentives have little impact on how many hours professionals choose to work, or where businesses locate their operations. The reality is the same principle applies.

We should be clear that saying "incentives matter" just reminds us of a *tendency* or a *force* that is in operation. In any individual case, a small change in incentives might not lead to a noticeable change in behaviour. Yet when even a small change in incentives is multiplied over *many* people, and over a long time frame, then the consequences can be surprising. For example, if a grocery store runs a "10% off" sale on hamburgers, this probably won't affect the behaviour of any customers who are vegetarians—they wouldn't have bought any hamburgers before, and they still won't. But the sale probably *will* affect the purchasing decisions of at least some of the other customers, so that when the meat department tallies its numbers at the end of the week, it will see a higher volume of hamburger sales than it otherwise would have expected.

The economist knows to check how incentives matter, even in unusual situations where others wouldn't expect such an influence. For example, suppose the Canadian government announces that it will impose a large "estate tax" (a tax on wealth transferred to heirs after death) in the coming calendar year. An economist might wonder if the reported death rate of elderly (and wealthy) patients in hospitals will spike in December, compared to the usual trends. In this scenario, the economist would conjecture that changing incentives—namely, by reducing how much of an estate one's heirs actually receive, once the new year begins—makes it financially advantageous for wealthy hospital patients to die on December 31, rather than January 1. If such an outcome *did* occur, the economist would then need to explore further, to determine the exact causes. (Did the patients themselves "let go" sooner? Did the hospital staff collude with families to alter the date of death on a few "close calls"? Did something more sinister happen?) The overarching point, however, is that *incentives matter*, and often in ways that would surprise the non-economist.

Economic Principle #2

There are always tradeoffs— there's no such thing as a free lunch

Economists often appear as the party poopers in public policy discussions, because they are the ones who point out that "there's no such thing as a free lunch." This popular expression simply means that there are always *tradeoffs*, that if we institute a new policy in order to make things better in one respect, we are probably making things worse in other respects. To point out the existence of tradeoffs doesn't reduce us to paralysis; it might make sense to go ahead with the change, even in light of the downsides. Yet it is crucial for people to understand *what the tradeoffs are* when they make decisions. When it comes to government policymakers in particular, economic analysis plays a critical role in highlighting the most serious drawbacks from a proposed change.

There are tradeoffs in all spheres of life. For example, if a mother rushes in to "rescue" her young child whenever he or she is about to make a mistake, this may actually stunt her child's social development. In a similar vein, if a college professor wants to be "nice" by always giving his students an "A," this too will be a fleeting gift because soon outsiders will recognize that the grade is meaningless. For yet another example, a business owner might try to be popular with his employees by having the vending machines in the company break room distribute free soft drinks and snacks during holidays or other special occasions. Yet one possible tradeoff from this policy is that the first employees to access the vending machines will quickly empty them, meaning that employees getting to the break room later in the shift find nothing available.

Taken literally, the economist's slogan, "There's no such thing as a free lunch," warns us that there is a resource cost to providing lunch whether or not you have to pay for it yourself. By a resource cost we mean someone

You have just won a free all-expenses
vacation. All you have to do is ....

had to pay for the bread, butter, and so forth, even if that someone was not you. So if an offer comes in the mail, for example, saying that the recipient is invited to a "free catered lunch" at a real estate agent's office, we can be sure that there is a pitch for a timeshare or other "opportunity" coming. *Somebody* has to pay for the lunch, and it often doesn't take much sleuthing to figure out why the offer exists.

Yet even though most citizens can exercise common sense and understand that there are no "free lunches" (whether literal or metaphorical) in the context of private businesses, for some reason citizens often seem to lose this healthy suspicion when it comes to promises made by government officials. Yet the principle holds for government action too: there are no free lunches. If the government mandates a new benefit, the economist has been trained to look for the tradeoff involved—a cut in some other government program, a tax or fee increase, increased public debt. To repeat, identifying the relevant tradeoffs doesn't mean that the policy is bad or unjustified; it just helps us make an informed decision.

For example, a research project from McGill University points out in a section titled, "Areas Where Canada Lags Behind":

> Out of 176 countries studied, 106 provide mothers with complete wage replacement during maternity leave. Although in a number of countries many women work in the informal sector, where these government guarantees do not always apply, the fact remains that most Canadian women are only guaranteed 55% of their insurable income during maternity leave. Women in Quebec fare a bit better, receiving 70 to 75% of their insurable income during maternity leave.[1]

Especially because of the section title (Canada "lags behind") and the statement that "[w]omen in Quebec fare a bit better," it is clear that these authors believe a federal mandate of *100%* pay during maternity leave would be a boon to women. Yet are there any tradeoffs involved? After all, someone must be paying for this "lunch."

---

1 See Martine Chaussard et al. (no date). *The Work Equity Canada Index: Where the Provinces and Territories Stand.* McGill University Institute for Health and Social Policy: 1. <http://www.mcgill.ca/ihsp/sites/mcgill.ca.ihsp/files/WorkEquityCanada.pdf>, as of July 8, 2014.

The most immediate party to lose from the new arrangement would be the employers of women taking maternity leave. It is expensive to continue paying full wages, even though the new mother isn't showing up to work while on leave. The employer will respond to this new situation in a host of ways, perhaps including raising product prices, cutting dividends to shareholders, and/or reducing compensation across the board in an attempt to mitigate the increased wage bill.

Yet there is an even more perverse possibility, which undercuts the idea that paid maternity legislation is a boon for women. Other things equal, the government mandate gives employers an incentive to *prefer hiring men (and older women) over young women*—particularly young and married women— who are most likely to exercise their legal option of full-paid maternity leave. Such a motivation wouldn't be directly due to sexism, but rather would be quite rational: With the mandate, young married women are in a position to impose higher expenses on the employer than men (or older women, or young, unmarried women who are focused on a career more than family). It would be naïve to expect employers *not* to react to this situation, especially if we look across the entire country and allow the mandate to remain in force for years.

Of course, there are other laws in place barring blatant discrimination. In response to the full-paid maternity mandate, an employer couldn't openly state, "We will not hire married women in their 20s." Yet the new mandate would still come with tradeoffs, perhaps showing up as a reduction in the compensation that certain women earned. (Thus, the employer would partly recover the expense of the full-paid maternity leave by reducing compensation costs on the front end.) To reiterate, this identification of the potential tradeoffs involved—pointing out that when it comes to maternity leave, there's no such thing as a free lunch—doesn't mean the policy is a bad idea. It *does* mean that Canadians need to think twice before "catching up" to the other countries that have already adopted such measures.

Economic Principle #3

People make decisions on the margin

When understanding and explaining the choices people make, economists recognize that the decisions are made *on the margin*. This phrase means that the choices only change things "at the edge"—think of the *margin* on a piece of paper—and they should be evaluated in this light. Some examples will help clarify the concept.

Suppose a grocery store is selling cans of beer for $1 each. We see a man start putting cans into his cart, obviously intending to take them to the register and buy them. At first we might be tempted to say, "Ah, this man values a can of beer more than a $1." Yet that can't be the whole story, because he eventually *stops* putting additional cans of beer into his cart. Assuming the man started with ten loonies in his wallet, the more accurate description would be, "The man thought the *first* can of beer was more valuable than the *tenth* loonie in his wallet. He also thought the second can of beer was more valuable than the ninth loonie, and likewise for the third can. However, he did *not* consider the fourth can of beer to be more valuable than his seventh loonie, and that's why he only put three total cans into his cart."

As the simple example of beer demonstrates, in economics we can't analyze people's decisions in terms of broad categories or classes; it won't work if we ask, "Does the man prefer cans of beer or loonies?" We need to engage in *marginal* analysis, and realize that the man will buy additional cans of beer until their "marginal cost" is higher than their "marginal benefit," at which point he will stop.

Another example of the importance of marginal thinking is the so-called "water-diamond paradox," an interesting puzzle famously discussed by Adam Smith. The alleged paradox is the high market value of diamonds, compared to water, when diamonds are a mere luxury item. In contrast, life itself depends on an adequate water supply. Why then are people prepared to pay so much more for, say, a kilogram of diamonds, than a kilogram of water?

Here again marginal thinking solves the problem. When someone is offered a choice between a diamond and a bottle of water, she is not choosing between *all diamonds* versus *all water*. Rather, she is being offered a choice between *this particular diamond* and *that particular bottle* of water. Thinking on the margin, in most cases and for most people, the additional diamond

All I want is a bottle of water.

would confer much greater *marginal benefits* than the additional bottle of water, and that's why most people would eagerly choose the diamond over a bottle of water. Now of course, in very unusual circumstances—such as a man crawling in the desert, who hasn't had a drink in hours—the choice might be flipped: The man could choose the water over the diamond because *that particular bottle* is indeed the difference between life and death. Once again, marginal analysis makes the solution obvious.

The failure to appreciate marginal thinking crops up in popular discussions over "excessive" pay. For example, people often complain that star hockey players make millions of dollars per year, while the average schoolteacher earns much less. "What does this say about our priorities as a nation?" goes the familiar cry.

Yet notice the similarity to the classical water-diamond paradox. Even though most (but perhaps not all!) Canadians would choose *all the schoolteachers* over *all the hockey players*, that's not the choice with which labour markets are confronted. In the real world, what happens is that *a particular individual* must decide whether to become a teacher at a certain school (versus some other occupation, or remaining unemployed), while another particular individual (with a very rare skill set) must decide whether to become a professional hockey player for a certain team. *On the margin*, any particular schoolteacher's services are not indispensable, since many Canadians have the aptitude (given suitable training) to become elementary schoolteachers. But not many people can become star hockey players. Thus, the market pays more for a year's worth of labour from a star hockey player than from an elementary schoolteacher, even though "education" broadly construed is far more important than "entertainment from professional sports." This is analogous to a diamond having a higher market price than a bottle of water, even though water in the grand scheme is far more important than jewelry.

Thinking on the margin helps us avoid falling prey to the "sunk cost" fallacy. For example, suppose a retailer invests $20,000 in order to stock his store with 1,000 artificial Christmas trees in the beginning of November. (Note that this implies an average cost of $20 per tree.) During the month of November and the first two weeks of December, the retailer charges his shoppers $25 per tree, making $5 profit on each unit sold. Yet as of December 15, the retailer still has 200 trees on his shelves and in the backroom, and he is worried that he will be stuck with them. He slashes the price from $25 down to $5, and puts up a big sign announcing the "fire sale" price. At the rock-bottom price, the retailer manages to sell all of the remaining trees by Christmas Eve.

In the above scenario, a critic might object that the retailer is acting foolishly by enacting the sale, since he's "losing $15" on every tree sold. (The retailer paid $20 per tree, yet only charged $5 on each of the final 200 units sold.) Yet this objection forgets that the $20,000 spent in acquiring the trees is already "sunk"; *no matter what* the retailer does, that $20,000 is already spent. The question is, *on the margin* what is the most profitable course? On December 15, if the retailer estimates that he only would have sold an additional 10 trees at the original price of $25, while he estimates selling out the remaining 200 trees by dropping the price to $5, then the latter course makes more sense. It has higher *marginal* benefits, because it brings in $1,000 in extra revenue compared to only $250 if the retailer refused to cut the price. Of course, since the retailer himself paid (on average) $20 per tree, he regrets buying so many trees initially; he would have made more profit had he only invested in 800 trees, not the full 1,000, in the beginning. Yet thinking on the margin means that *bygones are bygones*, and we must make the best of our current situation, realizing that we are powerless to alter our past behaviour.

Once our hypothetical retailer found himself in the scenario we described on December 15, he made more total profit by selling "below cost." Thinking on the margin illuminates the proper course of action.

Economic Principle #4

Voluntary trade is a win-win proposition (positive-sum game)

One of the beautiful aspects of the market is that it promotes a general harmony of interests, as the great 19th century classical liberal Frédéric Bastiat stressed in his writings. In other words, private enterprise doesn't produce winners and losers in the same way that a military confrontation, or even a simple poker game, does. These other scenarios involve zero-sum games, where one person's gain translates into someone else's loss, or even negative-sum games, where the total losses exceed the total gains. Such strategic environments pit people against each other, because their interests are fundamentally opposed.

Fortunately, private enterprise is not like that. It is a *positive-sum* game, where one person's gain can correspond to someone else's gain, too. Because of the underlying harmony of interests, the market fosters social bonds of cooperation. The market doesn't encourage people to engage in a pitiless war of all against all, but rather gives them incentives to work together for their mutual benefit. As the late Nobel laureate in economics Elinor Ostrom explained, economics and markets are about figuring out ways to cooperate with one another and by doing so coordinate our activities. This may seem a strange thing to say, given the negative connotations that the terms *markets* and *capitalism* have in the mind of the general public, but that's only because these critics ignore the voluntary nature of markets.

Fundamentally, "private enterprise" is a network of *voluntary exchanges* of property among the members of society. If we seek to make people happier *according to their own reckoning,* then voluntary trades are a great way to proceed. By definition, a voluntary trade means that both parties consented to the exchange. For example, suppose Bill has an apple for lunch while Sally has a banana. If Bill and Sally engage in a voluntary trade, then each person walks away better off, *in his or her own mind.* That is the straightforward, yet very important, sense in which voluntary trades are win-win scenarios.

Although the example may seem too mundane to be worth exploring further, this is a crucial point, so let's really analyze it thoroughly. Doesn't it seem strange that *both* people think they benefited from the trade? After all, it isn't possible for Bill and Sally each to walk away with the *heavier* piece of

fruit, or the piece of fruit with the most calories. Yet there *is* an important sense in which Bill can think, "I got the better piece of fruit out of that deal," while Sally can think the exact same thing.

The solution to our mystery is that *economic value is subjective.* In other words, when it comes to the benefits (and costs) of a decision, the weighing is ultimately done in the mind of the person involved, and such judgments can differ from person to person. There is nothing odd or irrational about Bill thinking that a banana is more desirable than an apple, while Sally thinks the opposite. This situation simply reflects the fact that economic value is subjective.

Because value is subjective, it is possible for the world to constantly become a happier place—two people at a time—through a series of voluntary trades. Whether we are looking at two students swapping fruit at lunch, or at investors buying steel to build a new factory, private enterprise is fundamentally built upon voluntary trades. Now it's true that people may make mistakes, and there are complications arising when two people may trade and disturb a third person without his consent. Even so, it is important to start with the basic fact that the economy is built upon a network of voluntary trades, a vast series of win-win propositions.

Notice, too, that voluntary trade doesn't just include the swapping of physical goods, but it also involves the sale of labour services. For example, if a homeowner pays the kid next door $15 to mow her lawn, this is a voluntary trade because (a) the homeowner values the cut lawn more than her initial $15, while (b) the kid next door values the $15 more than the leisure time he otherwise could have enjoyed. An outsider might object to the "exploitation" of the neighbour, and think it unfair for him to receive so little compensation, but because the trade was voluntary we know that the boy himself viewed it as a deal worth taking. Had the homeowner offered only, say, $5, the boy would have refused, choosing to watch TV instead.

It is only because of the possibility of trade that people can *specialize* in those areas in which they excel. Consider: if everyone had to eat only the food he grew or caught himself, and everyone had to wear only the clothes she herself produced, standards of living would be miserably low. But with trade, people are now free to produce far more of the particular goods or services in which they have the advantage. The farmer grows more potatoes than he can possibly eat, and sells most of his crop to others. Other people, in turn, "return the favour" by producing more automobiles, shorts, computers, and so forth, than they can personally use. This *division of labour* amplifies the initial difference in aptitudes that people have for various occupations, as years of training and practice only enhance their strengths. When every individual specializes in his or her area of excellence, the end result is a much larger total output, meaning higher standards of living across the board.

Economic Principle #5

People earn income and become wealthy by helping others

Because all transactions in a market economy must be voluntary, the only way to persuade others to give up their money is to *provide something that they value even more*. Whether it's a new hire at a fast food restaurant or the CEO of an international oil company, people earn their income by providing valuable services in the eyes of those who hire them. Regardless of the dollar amounts involved, the principle is the same.

The principle is clear enough when there are only two people directly involved in the transaction. For example, a street musician playing in downtown Toronto might receive tips in his open guitar case from passersby. In this scenario, it's obvious that his income is directly tied to the entertainment he provides to others.

Yet things get more complicated when we increase the scale of the operation. For example, if Céline Dion sings to a sell-out crowd in Toronto, she won't be getting paid *directly* from each of the thousands of fans. What happens instead, of course, is that her fans pay money to the ticket vendors, who take their cut and then hand the rest over to the promoters, who take their cut and also pay Dion the contractually specified amount. Notice that many of the people involved in this chain of transactions might not even care for her music. Yet she is still *indirectly* providing them with something they value—namely, ticket sales—and this is only possible because she *directly* provides the paying customers with valuable entertainment, in their eyes (and ears). Anybody can sing, but to become rich at it means convincing thousands, if not millions, of other people to attend concerts and buy albums.

If the way to earn income in a market economy is to help or to serve others, then the way to become wealthy is to consistently help a large number of people. To take just two familiar examples: New Brunswick brothers Harrison and Wallace McCain built their empire by pioneering the production and delivery of frozen French fries around the world, while Mike Lazaridis (whose family moved to Windsor from Turkey when he was 5) made his fortune by supplying busy professionals with a Blackberry, revolutionizing business communication. Especially with the ease of marketing and shipping in today's Internet-connected world, the budding entrepreneurs asked a simple question—"What good or service can I provide that millions of people *really* need or enjoy?"—and then found an answer.

This is the beauty and genius of private enterprise: it harnesses people's natural instinct for improving themselves and transforms it into a desire to serve others. As Adam Smith remarked, "It is not from the benevolence of the butcher, the brewer, or the baker, that we can expect our dinner, but from their regard to their own interest."[2]

Moreover, this ingenious arrangement *works*. As Smith famously explained: "By directing that industry in such a manner as its produce may be of greatest value, he intends only his own gain, and he is in this, as in many other cases, led by an invisible hand to promote an end which was no part of his intention."[3]

Critics of capitalism often lament the "market power" of those who "monopolize" industries, but we must never forget: All transactions in a genuinely free market are *voluntary*. Assuming he made his money legitimately in the market (as opposed to using fraud or threats, or getting special privileges from the government), a wealthy man must have delivered value in the eyes of many people. Indeed, part of the reason certain incomes—such as the earnings of celebrities and CEOs of particular companies—have risen so dramatically over the last few decades is that the rise of the Internet and other developments in global commerce have made it technically feasible for talented individuals to provide valuable services to hundreds of millions of people.

---

2 Adam Smith (1776). *An Inquiry Into the Nature and Causes of the Wealth of Nations*. Book I, Chapter 2, Paragraph 2.

3 Smith, Book IV, Chapter 2, Paragraph 9.

Economic Principle #6

Workers can only consume more if they first produce more

Before a man can eat a burger, someone first must have prepared the burger. Before a woman can eat an apple, someone first must have picked the apple. Before a child can play with a bicycle, someone first must have built the bicycle.

This seems pretty straightforward, and yet much of today's commentary on economic issues might cause Canadians to forget these obvious truths. Consider the following excerpt from a 2012 BNN story:

> The Canadian economy will be held back by belt-tightening governments and tapped-out consumers and will have to rely on its export sector and capital spending to support "mediocre" economic growth next year, according to CIBC economists.
>
> As such, CIBC has lowered its 2013 GDP forecast to 1.7% from its previous call of 2.0%.
>
> "Household debt burdens are keeping consumption bounded by the moderate growth pace for real incomes," CIBC Chief Economist Avery Shenfeld said in a note to clients on Wednesday. "Escaping economic mediocrity will depend on the kindness of strangers, with exports and related capital spending critical to Canada's fate in 2013-14."[4]

There is a danger, that when professional economists give pronouncements such as the one quoted above, the average Canadian begins thinking that *spending* actually drives economic growth, and that households could all enjoy greater consumption if they would simply go to the store and *buy more stuff*.

To avoid such erroneous conclusions, it's useful to review some basic facts. Before consumers can go to the mall and buy things, workers must have previously *produced* those very same items. Looking at the nation (or the

---

4 Brady Yauch (2012, December 19). Canada to Rely on Kindness of Strangers: CIBC. *Business News Network*. <http://www.bnn.ca/News/2012/12/19/CIBC-lowers-2013-GDP-forecast.aspx>, as of April 17, 2014.

world) as a whole, it is obvious that people can consume only what they have first produced. It's true, particular individuals might consume more than they produce—for example, toddlers eat food and wear clothing that they had no role in creating. Yet this is only possible because other people in society are consuming *less* food and clothing than they produced.

The standard of living in Canada today is much higher than in the year, say, 1800. Why is it that Canadians today can enjoy such a better material life than their forebears from centuries ago? The immediate answer is that Canadians today *produce more* when they go to work. That's what makes it physically possible for them to *consume more* when they go home or out on the town.

In a similar vein, Canadians today have a much higher standard of living than the people *today* living in Bangladesh and other developing countries. Again, the reason for this is simple: Canadian workers are more productive, that is they produce more per hour (or day, or year) than Bangladeshi workers currently can.

There are complications as we move from the aggregate, national level down to the individual. Typically, each person in her role as a consumer doesn't buy *exactly* the goods and services that she produces in her role as a worker. Rather, because of the benefits of specialization and trade (which we spelled out earlier), a worker will focus on producing large amounts of a few things in which she has expertise, in order to earn money with which she then goes into the market to buy small amounts of the many things she wants to consume. Yet even here, it is still true that *measured in terms of money* and *in the long run*, an individual can ultimately only take out of the market as a consumer what he contributes to it as a worker.[5, 6]

---

5 We are ignoring the complication that not everyone in society is solely a "worker," relying on his or her labour as the only source of income. For example, some people own oil deposits, agricultural land, and other forms of natural resources, which they can sell or rent to others for money. In addition, many people either directly or indirectly (through their retirement plans) own shares of corporate stock, bonds, machinery, and other forms of financial and physical capital, which they can sell or rent for money. Yet these complications don't affect the spirit of our basic principle, because such "landowners" and "capitalists" can only consume what their property contributes to total output.
6 People may often consume less than what they produce, by saving the difference and accumulating a stockpile of assets. If they die before consuming them, then their heirs can continue to hold the wealth, or they can decide to "live above their means" by consuming it. Even here, total (or per-capita) consumption can't be higher than total (or per-capita) income. At best, some people in the earlier generation can consume less than they produce, so that some people in the later generation can consume more.

After clarifying the context, our economic principle is clear: Workers can only consume more if they first produce more. If we want Canadians to have a higher standard of living—to be able to buy more stuff—we must find ways to make Canadians more *productive*. Narrowly focusing on the immediate transactions, and observing that "spending money" goes hand in hand with a sale, can mislead us into thinking that the way to boost economic growth is to give Canadian consumers (or even foreign consumers) more money. Yet the mere spending of money is incidental. Without the necessary technological and institutional prerequisites for increased production, more spending by domestic and foreign consumers by itself will only lead to higher prices for the same quantity of physical output.

Government policies to improve the material well-being of Canadians—such as access to food, medical care, transportation, and education—will, at best, merely *rearrange* consumption if they do nothing to increase the average level of worker productivity. Indeed, most government policies are actually *harmful* in this respect, because they alter the incentives that individual workers face. If the most productive are penalized (by having some of their output taken) while the least productive are subsidized (by being given the output taken from the first group), we should not be surprised to see a decline in total work effort from *both* groups. This is because incentives matter: by reducing the reward for work, and mitigating the harm of not working, many people will quite rationally choose to work less than they otherwise would have. Therefore, the total pie becomes smaller, meaning government efforts to increase the consumption of certain groups result in a larger decline in consumption of other groups, as total production—and hence total consumption—falls.

As with the discussion of our other principles, these remarks do not eliminate the case for government assistance for the needy. Nonetheless, it is essential to understand the sources of economic prosperity, so that well-meaning efforts to help the poor do not unwittingly impoverish everyone.

Economic Principle #7

Saving and investment today allow for greater prosperity in the future

The previous principle explained that the *most* a country can consume is all that it produces. But if its citizens collectively consume *less* than they produce, they will lay the foundation for greater production—and therefore consumption—down the road.

Everyone can recognize the tradeoff involved with saving at the household level. Suppose a brother and sister, Harry and Mary, each earns $100,000 in salary, and (to keep things simple) they never get a raise. Further suppose Harry always consumes his entire paycheck, buying $100,000 worth of goods and services throughout the year. Notice that Harry will never get ahead financially; he will always consume $100,000 per year, and when he retires he will be destitute, having to rely on support from others.

In contrast, suppose his sister Mary always *saves* 20% (a fifth) of her income. The first year, she is at a disadvantage compared to Harry. She spends only $80,000 on food, housing, transportation, clothes, entertainment, and so on, meaning that she doesn't go out to as many restaurants, she lives in a smaller apartment, she drives an uglier car, and so on. Her lifestyle is definitely not as fun as Harry's, at least at the moment. With the other $20,000 from her paycheck, Mary buys a bank certificate of deposit (CD) earning 5% annually.

Now, because of their different savings decisions, the second year is not merely a repeat of the first. Harry still earns his $100,000 base pay, and blows it all on present enjoyments, just as before. But now Mary has seen her total income go up. Like her brother, she still earns $100,000 in salary, but her CD holdings generate an additional $1,000 (= $20,000 x 5%) in interest income. Because Mary always puts aside a fifth of her total income, this second year she spends $80,800 on consumption and adds another $20,200 to her CD portfolio (bringing her total wealth up to $40,200).

Neglecting taxes and other complications, in our simple scenario Mary will, by the 24th year, have accumulated assets worth more than half a million dollars. Because these assets generate so much additional income to be combined with her base salary, in this critical year Mary will be able—even after she sets aside a fifth in new savings—to outspend her brother on food, entertainment, and other goodies. From this point forward, Mary will have a higher standard of living than her brother, and her advantage will grow exponentially. What's more, when she retires and stops earning a paycheck, Mary will have a very large amount of wealth in the form of bank CDs, which she can begin selling off to meet her expenses as she continues eating at her favourite restaurants and even takes the occasional vacation cruise. Far from being a financial burden on others—like her penniless brother—in her older years Mary will actually be a financial benefactor, sending her grandkids birthday presents and leaving a sizable inheritance when she dies.

The pattern at the individual, household level is clear: Embracing a high rate of saving will mean a reduction in one's "lifestyle," at least in the short run. But as these savings are invested into productive assets (rather than unproductive assets like plasma-screen TVs and sports cars), total income grows over time, meaning that consumption spending can rise as well. Eventually, the person who saves a large fraction of her income can spend more than would have been possible on a trajectory that involved no saving. Thus, saving and investment brings short-term pain, but long-term gain, in obvious financial terms at the individual household level.

This pattern holds true at the national level, too. If *Canadians as a whole* decide to save a larger fraction of their income, this will cause an immediate drop in total consumption spending. But the correspondingly higher investment spending will lead to faster GDP growth than otherwise would have occurred. Eventually, Canadians will enjoy a higher standard of living—forever—than would have been possible with the original, lower level of saving.

To understand the engineering realities behind this pattern, keep in mind that there are many different combinations of goods and services that an economy can produce, with its available supplies of natural resources, labour power, and capital equipment. If the citizens spend the vast bulk of their incomes on present enjoyments, their financial decisions will be mirrored by an economy full of restaurants, retail shopping centres, and movie theaters. Such an economy would have factories, but they would be churning out sports cars and romance novels. The productivity of workers in such a world would not rise very quickly, because most of the new equipment being produced would simply replace the worn-out equipment catering to consumers.

In contrast, if the citizens save a large fraction of their income, their financial decisions will be mirrored by an economy full of fertilizer plants, research laboratories, and offshore oil platforms probing the ocean floor. The factories in this economy would crank out tractor trailers and physics textbooks. Because each year would bring a wave of new tools and equipment, as well as a rapid rate of technological advancements, the productivity of workers would rise very rapidly. Eventually, the workers would be so productive that even the smaller fraction of their economy devoted to consumption goods would still imply a larger *absolute* output of consumer goods for everyone to enjoy.

Whether looking at the individual household in financial terms, or at the entire national economy in physical or "real" terms, the principle is the same: Saving and investment today allow for greater prosperity in the future.

Economic Principle #8

Prices provide valuable information to buyers and sellers

Although we often take it for granted, private enterprise achieves tremendous feats of coordination, day in and day out. In an advanced nation like Canada, when a household runs out of milk, the teenage son might be dispatched to the grocery store to obtain more. Everyone involved simply *assumes* that there will be rows upon rows of fresh, packaged milk, waiting there for the boy. (Think about how much planning and work *just this* required—not only from the dairy farmers but the engineers who designed the refrigeration units, the truck drivers who delivered the product to the store, and the grocery store employees who stocked the dairy cooler.) When he grabs the milk and walks to the checkout line, the boy further just *assumes* that there will be someone there, waiting to ring him out. And of course, if the boy used a car to make the trip, that required not only thousands of people who previously worked to create it, but also the untold people involved in extracting petroleum, refining it into gasoline, and delivering it to the local gas station so that the family car could continue making trips to the store.

In the 19th century, Frédéric Bastiat summed it up this way, in his discussion of a student:

> What is he doing in Paris? How does he live? No one can deny that society puts at his disposal food, clothing, lodging, amusements, books, instruction—such a host of things, in a word, that it would take a long time just to tell how they were produced, to say nothing of actually producing them. And in return for all these things that have demanded so much work, the sweat of so many brows, so much painful toil, so much physical or mental effort, such prodigies of transportation, so many inventions, transactions, what services has our student rendered society? None; but he is getting ready to render them. How, then, can these millions of men who are engaged in positive, effective, and productive work turn over to him the fruit of their labour? Here is the explanation: This student's father, who was a doctor or a lawyer or a businessman, had already rendered services—perhaps to Chinese

society—and had received in return, not immediate services, but certificates for services due him on which he could demand payment at the time and place and in the form that he saw fit. Today society is paying for those distant and past services; and, amazingly, if we were to follow in our minds the chain of endless transactions that had to take place before the final result was reached, we should see that each one was paid for his pains; that these certificates passed from hand to hand, sometimes split up into fractions, sometimes combined into larger sums, until by our student's consumption the full account was balanced. Is not this indeed a most remarkable phenomenon?[7]

It's worth dwelling on this "most remarkable phenomenon" identified by Bastiat. In a private enterprise system, people have the ability to choose their occupations without being ordered from on high. At the same time, individuals have the freedom to choose what types of breakfast cereal they will eat, whether they will drive a car or truck (or use a bicycle), and so on. Yet superimposed on all of this freedom must be a reality-check: There are always tradeoffs, as we know, and if everybody tries to become a professional athlete, then there will be no one to grow food or pick up the garbage. Further, the more of society's scarce resources that are channeled into automobiles, the less is available for producing diapers and sweaters. If individuals in their role as workers are allowed to pick whatever job they want, and individuals in their role as consumers are allowed to buy whatever goods and services they want, then how can we ensure that all of their plans will mesh? How can we make such a seemingly anarchic system *work*?

The short answer is that *market prices* provide a valuable source of information that guides both buyers and sellers. First, let's think about the impact of market prices on sellers. Intuitively, the higher the price for a certain type of labour or finished product, the more scarce it is; at least some members of society are "voting with their dollars" to say that this type of labour or good is very important and other people should really think about providing more of it.

---

7 Frédéric Bastiat (1850/1996). Chapter 1: Natural and Artificial Social Order. *Economic Harmonies*. George B. de Huszar (trans.) and W. Hayden Boyers (ed.). Foundation for Economic Education. <http://www.econlib.org/library/Bastiat/basHar1.html>, as of May 27, 2013.

Still a kid at
heart, huh?

Nah, this is a
collector's item.
I bet I can get $25
for this on e-Bay.

A young man in his late teens might very well envision becoming a hockey star or a famous musician, and nobody can *force* him to abandon his dream. But at the same time, he in turn can't force a hockey team to add him to the roster, and he can't force people in the music industry to distribute his songs. Everything in the market place must be voluntary. Prices help communicate where people's talents will best be directed. Perhaps the young man can't get hired as an athlete or musician, but he has a quick mind, loves numbers, and is very organized. Seeing the relatively high salaries earned by accountants right out of college, the young man embarks on a more realistic career path.

Market prices guide the decisions of buyers, as well. Perhaps a woman would love to eat nothing but filet mignon and sushi every night for dinner; in a free society, no government agency can dictate to her what her meals must be. Yet by the same token, she can't compel the various ranchers, fishermen, and chefs involved to slave away to provide her with a stream of exquisite meals—they all must be offered enough money to make it worth their while. Seeing the relative prices of filet mignon versus hamburger meat, and sushi versus frozen fish sticks, the woman adopts a more reasonable course of action. She only *occasionally* goes out for expensive meals, in order to devote her available income to other goals besides food.

Thus, we see that market prices communicate valuable information to both buyers and sellers.[8] In a free market economy, individuals are free to choose their occupations and can purchase whatever types of goods and services they want. However, budgets impose discipline on this freedom—people can't spend more than they earn (at least not in the long run). The wages or salaries offered by various jobs, and the prices attached to various items for sale, help guide people in making their decisions in a way that reflects the desires of others, as well as the physical constraints imposed by the scarcity of resources and technological know-how.

Economic Principle #9

Profits harness self-interest to guide entrepreneurs in using scarce resources efficiently

Critics of private enterprise often lament that businesses only serve the "bottom line." A popular slogan demands that our institutions cater to "people, not profits." Indeed, the very terms *capitalism* and *socialism* were adopted by Karl Marx (and other early socialists) in order to imply that a capitalist system serves only the narrow interests of the capitalists, while a socialist system serves all of society.

Yet with our earlier principles in hand, we can now see the emptiness of such typical characterizations. Contrary to popular belief, in a market economy profits are a mechanism to guide entrepreneurs—acting in their self-interest—to use scarce resources efficiently. Generally speaking, it's a *good thing* when a business turns a profit, because it's a signal that the people running it have channeled scarce resources into the areas where they are most needed.

---

8 In formal economics classes, the student will learn that in the real world, market prices do not convey all of the information required for decision-makers to act perfectly efficiently, judged from a theoretical ideal. Many economists believe that such imperfection in markets gives scope for government corrective measures. However, in the text above we are merely sketching out the basic process whereby prices guide behaviour and help bring order to the market, "solving" a problem day in and day out that at first defies comprehension.

To see why earning a profit is actually a sign of social benefit, we need to drop the socialist imagery of the landowners and captains of industry as the people "in charge" of the economy. Even though they superficially run the show, they too must ultimately answer to their superiors: their own customers. As von Mises put it:

> The capitalists, the enterprisers, and the farmers are instrumental in the conduct of economic affairs. They are at the helm and steer the ship. But they are not free to shape its course. They are not supreme, they are steersmen only, bound to obey unconditionally the captain's orders. The captain is the consumer. …

> The real bosses [under capitalism] are the consumers. They, by their buying and by their abstention from buying, decide who should own the capital and run the plants. They determine what should be produced and in what quantity and quality. Their attitudes result either in profit or in loss for the enterpriser. They make poor men rich and rich men poor. They are no easy bosses. They are full of whims and fancies, changeable and unpredictable. They do not care a whit for past merit. As soon as something is offered to them that they like better or is cheaper, they desert their old purveyors.[9]

In a private enterprise system, the entrepreneurs stand in between the final consumers on the one hand, and the resource owners (the workers, the owners of farmland and oil deposits, the owners of factories and equipment, etc.) on the other hand. The entrepreneurs must make decisions on what quantities of various inputs—labour, natural resources, and capital equipment—to buy, in order to produce goods and services for sale to their customers.

Through it all, the entrepreneurs are guided by market prices, but specifically by their expectation of profit: The entrepreneur will embark on a path only if she thinks that the total amount of money she will raise from her customers is more than the total amount she must spend on the labour and other inputs needed to create the product or service.

---

9 Ludwig von Mises (1944). *Bureaucracy*. Ludwig von Mises Institute: 226–227.
<http://mises.org/etexts/mises/bureaucracy/section1.asp>, as of April 17, 2014.

*I think we could have found
a better use for that champagne.*

These features of private entreprise, where prices are attached to every item of inputs and outputs, and where entrepreneurs operate within this system looking to make a profit, give rise to the orderly outcome at which Bastiat marveled. If an entrepreneur is to be profitable, it's not enough that she produces something that her customers want. No, she must go further and produce something that her customers want, *without using up scarce resources that could've been used to make something that other customers would want even more.* The economic question is not merely *what* a given firm should make, but *how* the firm should make it.

To understand this subtle yet crucial point, consider an exaggerated example. Suppose a developer wants to build a 20-story apartment complex, where the walls and furniture of each unit are coated in gold. The developer points out that just about everybody would love to live in such an apartment; after all, the pharaohs of Egypt and other rulers of antiquity chose to live in such luxury. Why not do the same today for the people living in apartments in downtown Montreal?

Of course, we can recognize immediately that this proposal is absurd. It would be incredibly *wasteful* to coat an apartment building with gold, even though the people living in the building would enjoy the perk. In a private enterprise system, such a foolish idea would get nipped in the bud when the developer's accountant pointed out how *unprofitable* it would be. It's true, the developer would be able to charge higher rents for units coated with gold, versus units coated with paint or wallpaper. That would reflect the preference of the tenants to live in apartments coated with gold, versus more conventional choices.

Yet even though the developer could boost his rental revenue by using gold, his *costs* would skyrocket far more, because gold has such a higher market price than paint or wallpaper. The net effect of the large rise in revenue but the astronomical increase in expenses would mean a sharp drop in profitability. This is the sense in which profit-and-loss accounting, which is based on market prices, helps guide entrepreneurs when they make decisions on what to provide for their customers.

We can push the analysis further, however, to see the social significance of this outcome. *Why* is gold so much more expensive than paint or wallpaper? The answer is that there are *other* entrepreneurs in the market, who are themselves bidding on the scarce supplies of gold. Specifically, there are jewelers using gold to make necklaces, earrings, and other ornamental items. There are also entrepreneurs willing to pay the market price to obtain gold for medicinal and industrial purposes, and also to produce coins and bullion. It *is* profitable for these entrepreneurs to use gold in their operations, and that's why they are able to do so in a free enterprise system.

As this example illustrates, it's not enough to focus on the business that refrains from a certain operation—whether coating apartment units with gold, or providing more baby formula for mothers—and lament that the profit system has stifled production. On the contrary, *all* of society's resources are up for grabs; if *no* business could afford to use a particular resource, then its owners would have to slash prices if they wanted to earn any income.

The profit and loss system doesn't stifle output in general, it merely ensures that scarce resources get channeled into the *appropriate* lines of production. If an entrepreneur suffers losses, it's the market's way of telling him that he squandered resources that consumers wish had been devoted elsewhere. When an entrepreneur enjoys a large profit, the market is announcing that she discovered a better way to use scarce resources.

It's important to remember that when it comes to business, private enterprise doesn't respect past accomplishments; the entrepreneurs must continually earn the loyalty of their customers, week in and week out. Even large companies that dominate their respective industries can only maintain their position of strength by vigilantly altering their products or services and by staying ahead of the competition. Every industry is always susceptible to the gales of what economist Joseph Schumpeter called "creative destruction," in which a bold innovator introduces a new product or technique and disrupts the old ways of doing business.[10]

Economic Principle #10

Policymakers must consider the long-term and "unseen" consequences of their actions

In his famous book *Economics In One Lesson*, Henry Hazlitt (echoing the wisdom of Bastiat) wrote:

> [T]he whole of economics can be reduced to a single lesson, and that lesson can be reduced to a single sentence. *The art of economics consists in looking not merely at the immediate but at the longer effects of any act or policy; it consists in tracing the consequences of that policy not merely for one group but for all groups.* (Emphasis in original.)[11]

We have already seen this principle in operation in our earlier discussion on the unseen or unintended consequences of legislation mandating that employers pay workers for extended periods while they take maternity leave. Although superficially this sounds like a "pro-women" measure, it could paradoxically achieve the opposite result, making it harder for young women to find work and/or reducing their average earnings. As Hazlitt notes, it is the job of economists to inform the public of such consequences whenever a politician proposes some apparently beneficial new policy.

This outcome is not unusual, in which government measures ostensibly designed to help particular groups ironically end up hurting them. For example, if the government offers tax credits, vouchers, or other forms of

---

10 Joseph A. Schumpeter (1942). Chapter 7: Process of Creative Destruction. *Capitalism, Socialism and Democracy*. HarperPerennial: 81–86.

11 Henry Hazlitt (1946) [1979]. *Economics in One Lesson*. Crown Publishers: 17.

If you don't mind, I won't be rushing to get us there.

financial assistance to poor, single parents in proportion to the number of dependent children, this could perversely provide incentives for behaviour that will only perpetuate poverty. Even if such an outcome is not the intent of the policymakers implementing the programs, they must be realistic in assessing the long-run unintended consequences of such programs.

For a different example, Gerald Wilde—a controversial researcher at the Psychology Department at Queens University who has been favourably cited by bestselling author Malcolm Gladwell—has long urged policymakers to consider that motorists may rationally alter their driving behaviour in response to changes in road conditions and vehicle attributes (such as seat belts, airbags, better braking, etc.). Wilde has offered a "risk compensation theory" or "risk homeostasis theory" which argues that drivers have different, subjective levels of both accident risk tolerance and desire for mobility. Paradoxically, it is possible that "traffic calming devices" such as speed bumps could actually be counterproductive for safety, because they reduce mobility while doing nothing directly to reduce drivers' tolerance for accidents.[12] Wilde's theoretical and empirical work shows that even something as mundane as road design must take into account the impact of incentives and the unintended consequences of policy changes.

---

12 Gerald J. S. Wilde (2001). *Target Risk 2.* PDE Publications.

For a final example, we can discuss an issue that economists have studied very extensively: rent control. With rent control laws, the government imposes a *price ceiling* on the legally permissible rent that a landlord can charge a tenant (i.e. a maximum rent). The obvious rationale for such policies is to provide affordable housing for poor and middle class renters, but in practice these are the very people who are hurt by the policy. To see why, let's walk through a hypothetical example.

Suppose that the market would normally set the rent of an apartment of a certain size and location in Ottawa for $1000 per month. By definition, if $1000 is the market price, it balances the opposing forces of supply and demand, so that owners of apartment units want to fill the same number of units that tenants want to occupy.

Now, if the Ottawa city council passes an ordinance capping the rent on such apartments at $850 per month, several undesirable consequences will follow. First and most immediate, there will be a *shortage* in available apartment units. At the original price, the quantity supplied by landlords and the quantity demanded by tenants were roughly equal. But at the lower price, more tenants are trying to find apartments—after all, they're cheaper. At the same time, the owners of apartment units do not want to offer as many on the market. For example, people who owned houses and had been willing to rent out a spare bedroom for $1000 per month, may now decide that it's not worth the hassle of interviewing potential tenants, having a stranger come and go, not having an empty room if out of town guests arrive, and so forth. Put the two facts together—an increased quantity demanded but a decreased quantity supplied—and you have a shortage. There are now lots of Ottawa residents willing to rent an apartment for $850 per month, but they have a very hard time finding any vacancies.

There are other, perverse consequences as well. Now that the local government has artificially capped prices, it is less profitable for real estate developers to build more apartment buildings. Thus, not only does rent control lead to an immediate shortage, but it also stifles the long-run construction of new apartment units. This can be particularly damaging in a city with rapid population growth.

Finally, rent control gives rise to a class of people who are dubbed "slumlords" in the vernacular. By preventing landlords from charging what the market will bear, rent control changes the business model for successful management of apartments. It no longer makes sense for a landlord to cater to his customers (i.e. the tenants) by fixing the water heater or elevator at 3 a.m. Instead, because the rent control has capped prices but created a queue of new tenants waiting for a vacancy, the incentives are now for a landlord to minimize his maintenance expenses and to disregard customer satisfaction. There is no reason to put on a new coat of paint periodically, or to replace the burned-out light bulbs in the building foyer, if the landlord will be assured of full occupancy in any event. Perversely, rent control makes it a wise business decision for sympathetic, tenderhearted landlords to sell their buildings to gruff and merciless "slumlords."

As we continue through this book, we will encounter ever more examples of this final principle: Policymakers must consider the long-run and "unseen" consequences of their actions.

CHAPTER TWO

Institutional prerequisites essential for economic progress

Institutions matter

In Chapter One we outlined ten principles of sound economic thinking. In the present chapter, we will explore seven institutional prerequisites for a prosperous economy. Now that we know how to "think like an economist," we can see that institutions, or what some economists call the "rules of the game," really do matter.

Institutions provide the context and rules within which individuals and businesses conduct their affairs. An entertaining and successful sporting event requires more than just talented athletes; it also requires sensible rules that are enforced by impartial judges (sometimes referred to as referees or umpires, depending on the sport). In the same way, modern economies rely on more than just skilled workers and eager investors. They also require, for instance, a sensible legal structure enforced by impartial judges. Yet economists have discovered other institutional prerequisites for prosperity, which we will outline in this second chapter.

Policymakers can either work to augment the market or to hamper it. As we will see, there are many reasons to prefer voluntary market exchanges as the default mechanism for allocating resources, as opposed to top-down planning by government officials. An economy based on enterprise has the power to reduce poverty, improve working conditions, and increase living standards, but only if it is allowed properly function.

Institutional Prerequisite #1

An unbiased legal system

In Chapter One we discussed the many benefits of a market economy, including mutual gains from trade, greater productivity through specialization, and rising living standards from capital accumulation. Yet our entire discussion took for granted the security of individuals in their property and persons. Market economies can only work if the legal system recognizes legitimate property titles, and the courts enforce contracts in an evenhanded manner. Indeed, the bedrock concept underlying a market economy—voluntary exchange—doesn't even make *sense* without such an institutional framework, because a "voluntary" exchange is one in which the legitimate owner's wishes are respected.

Imagine working for an employer if there were no guarantee that the contract you signed with her would be enforced in court. On the other hand, imagine being an employer where judges always ruled in favour of employees, making it impossible to fire them, even if they repeatedly failed to show up for work. These extreme examples underscore the importance of an unbiased legal framework.

Beyond the protection of property rights—a topic to which we will return shortly—an unbiased legal system is essential for what people mean by the term "rule of law." In a market-oriented society, citizens need not fear arbitrary imprisonment for vaguely defined infractions. Beyond the obvious justice of an evenly enforced criminal code, it also allows citizens the safety to criticize the government and other powerful individuals (such as the owners of large corporations), without fear of official punishment. This is a healthy feature of an open society that gives rise to a "free press" and a well-informed citizenry.

Although the need for a functioning and fair legal system is obvious in the abstract, in practice governments routinely fail to live up to this standard. For example, in many countries—particularly in Latin America and Africa—tourists and local businessmen have learned that the only way to get things done is to offer a bribe to the correct government official. Besides such petty corruption, there are more extreme examples of governments "nationalizing" entire industries outright—a euphemism for seizing the property of others.

Indeed, one of the puzzles of economics is why capital doesn't flow to areas in Africa and other labour-intensive regions, when in theory the capital should earn a high rate of return. One major explanation is that foreign investors cannot be assured that their property will be safe. Short of outright nationalization, a common practice is that the local government will enact "currency controls" and make it difficult to move profits out of the foreign country. It does little good to a Canadian investor to know that he is earning 30% on his money, if he must hold it indefinitely in the form of Nigerian naira.

Even in economically advanced countries with limited, constitutional governments, property rights are often not secure. For example, in Canada (primarily through provincial government legislation) there are legal penalties for interfering with species that are considered endangered or at risk. Although the goal of such legislation is, of course, praiseworthy, overly aggressive penalties could have a chilling effect on development. Investors will be less inclined to buy a piece of unused land and turn it into a shopping centre or housing development, when they know that a migratory bird in six months could bring the project to a screeching halt. In such a circumstance, even though the investors would still be the technical owners of the real estate, in reality their property rights would have been greatly neutered.

Evenhanded enforcement of contracts is also crucial for a prosperous nation. For example, suppose a contract between an insurance company and a homeowner promises to indemnify the owner in case of property damage, *except* for catastrophic "acts of God." Further suppose that a tornado rips through the town, and happens to demolish this particular house. The homeowner then sues the insurance company, arguing that he should be made whole, even though the contract specifically ruled out liability in such cases. If the legal system decides to ignore the clear language of the contract and award damages out of "compassion for the little guy," this will have unintended consequences. Insurance companies will realize that they can't rely on their actual contracts, and will have to tell their actuaries to adjust their calculations in light of the huge payouts for which they may now be on the hook. Insurers will either exit the industry, stop issuing policies to homeowners in areas prone to natural disasters (such as floods, earthquakes, tornadoes, etc.), and/or raise premiums for all policyholders to cover the increase in expected payouts. When the economy adjusts to the new legal precedent, the result will not simply be a transfer of wealth from the "rich insurance companies" to suffering homeowners, but also will degrade the efficiency of the insurance sector itself, and may even make it impossible for some poorer homeowners to obtain basic coverage.

In a related vein, unreasonably large damage awards for lawsuits against "deep pockets" can also cripple the smooth functioning of an economy. A famous example is the 1994 United States court case in which a jury awarded $2.7 million in punitive damages and $200,000 in compensatory damages (reduced to $160,000)[13] to an elderly woman who suffered third-degree burns after she spilled a cup of McDonald's coffee in her lap. (The trial judge later reduced the punitive damages to $480,000.)[14] If large, profitable companies know they are vulnerable to such outcomes, they will be forced to retain expensive legal teams and take out large insurance policies; these extra costs of business will ultimately be passed on to their customers. Such trends are the motivation behind "tort reform" movements. Fortunately, this particular issue is not as severe in Canada as in other countries. Indeed, one legal blogger posted a picture of a retailer's Styrofoam cup reading, "If this was another country, we'd have to tell you this coffee may be hot. Good thing this is Canada!"[15]

If the government at times violates the property rights of large companies in a misguided effort to help the modest individual, it also can err in the opposite direction, by trampling on the property rights of the small homeowner. For example, the 1997 Supreme Court case *Hill v. Nova Scotia* involved the provincial government expropriating (the actual legal term) land in order to construct a highway that bisected the Hill farm.[16] There are safeguards in place that insist the property owners are compensated when "public interest" projects (allegedly) require the expropriation of their land, but the entire topic would be moot if the government had to convince owners to voluntarily *sell*

---

13 New York Law School Center for Justice and Democracy (no date). McDonalds' Hot Coffee Case—Read the Facts Not the Fiction. Texas Trial Lawyers Association. <https://www.ttla.com/index.cfm?pg=McDonaldsCoffeeCaseFacts>, as of April 10, 2014.
14 New York Law School Center for Justice and Democracy (no date).
15 Lawhaha.com (2012, November 13). Warning: Canadian Coffee Seller Makes Fun of Hot Coffee Warnings. <http://lawhaha.com/warning-canadian-coffee-seller-makes-fun-of-hot-coffee-warnings/>, as of April 10, 2014.
16 See *Hill v. Nova Scotia (Attorney General)* (1997). *Judgments of the Supreme Court of Canada*. Lexum. <http://scc.lexum.org/decisia-scc-csc/scc-csc/scc-csc/en/item/1466/index.do> as of April 10, 2014.

their property. If the government can build a highway through someone's land without his consent—even if it "compensates" him—it is clear that his ownership rights are diminished, and the incentives to develop the land are smaller than they otherwise would be.

Although the situation in this country is much better than in many others around the world, even so it is important for Canadians to recognize that an unbiased legal system is a crucial institution for economic prosperity, as well as for civil liberties and political rights that underpin what most people consider a "free society."

These assertions are backed up by the empirical evidence, too. For example, Feldmann (2009a) uses data from 75 countries from 1995 to 2003, and uses statistical analysis to conclude that a legal system characterized by a dependent judiciary, biased courts, and other indicators of a weak rule of law tends to have substantially higher unemployment rates, particularly among young people.

Institutional Prerequisite #2

Limited government regulations

If a prosperous economy needs a legal system with well-defined and fairly enforced property rights, it also requires limited government regulations. A government regulation is a rule (backed by the force of law) that "regulates" the legal manner in which people can behave and use their property. Citizens might still be the legally recognized owner of a piece of property—such as a field or a factory—but the government *regulates* how they may use it.

The rationale for government regulation is to improve the operation of markets. However, in practice government regulation may be too prescriptive and become excessive, the proverbial "cure worse than the disease."

Excessive government regulation raises the costs of doing business, which reduces wages, increases consumer prices, and weakens the incentives for entrepreneurs to innovate. Because regulations force individuals and businesses to alter their behaviour—otherwise there would be no point to issuing the regulations—they result in lower total economic output. These burdens of government regulation are often hidden, with their true cost not visible in the same way that tax revenues flowing to the government are obvious and tangible.

The burden imposed on businesses from government regulations include the out-of-pocket expenses of directly satisfying the requirement. For example, if the government insists that all businesses of a certain type need wheelchair-accessible entrance ramps, then the businesses that otherwise would *not* have provided such ramps will obviously need to spend the extra money to obtain them. In this example, the new rule will make it easier for wheelchair-bound citizens to enter the affected businesses, but there's no such thing as a free lunch: The higher costs will reduce output and lead to higher prices for everyone, including those in wheelchairs. To justify this, one would need to offer a specific argument for why the political process would yield a better answer to the question of the correct number of wheelchair ramps than the decentralized competitive marketplace, in which business owners try to attract as large a clientele as possible while watching the bottom line.

Another aspect of the burden imposed by government regulations is termed *compliance costs*. These include the money spent on lawyers, accountants, and other professionals in order to fill out the paperwork and perform other tasks to prove to the government that a business has satisfied government regulations. There is also the opportunity cost of all of the *time* that business owners as well as individual citizens devote to regulatory compliance. For example, if a homeowner must get permission from a local zoning board to, say, add a shed to his backyard, he may end up making several phone calls and reading online explanations of the rules, devoting hours to the task over and above whatever he might pay an attorney to fill out the relevant paperwork.

In the extreme, as regulations proliferate, business owners and individuals alike can find themselves trapped, in which it may be truly impossible to conduct normal affairs *without* being in technical violation of some open-ended and vaguely worded code. In such an environment, government officials assume quite arbitrary power, as they have the ability to discover some type of "infraction" and penalize anyone whom the regime finds inconvenient. Not only is this outcome economically inefficient in narrow material terms, but it also violates the cherished principle of the rule of law.

Economist Hernando de Soto sought to understand why some nations lag behind in economic development, despite untold billions in foreign assistance and consultation with various experts from around the world. One of

his major conclusions was that excessive business regulations could cripple the human drive for entrepreneurship. Most of the lucky residents of developed countries with relatively tame government bureaucracies have no idea of how bad it can be:

> When Hernando de Soto began studying the possibility of giving the poor access to formal property in Peru during the 1980s, every major law firm he consulted assured him that setting up a formal business would only take a few days. De Soto figured that might be true for him and other people that had resources and connections, but he had a hunch it was not true for the majority of Peruvians.
>
> As an experiment, he decided to set up a two-sewing machine shop in a Lima shantytown. He hired two young women and put them under the supervision of someone who knew what steps were needed. Then, they listed and timed each and every step it took for a typical entrepreneur to get through all of the red tape and paperwork. They included time spent on buses and waiting in lines.
>
> They discovered that to legally set up this tiny business, it took more than 300 days working six hours a day. The cost was more than 32 times the minimum wage. In the U.S., it takes just a few weeks and can cost less than $1,000 in most states.

In every country in which de Soto and the Institute for Liberty and Democracy (ILD) work, they do a similar study of the bureaucratic steps, costs and time it takes the average person legally to open a small business or to get title to land. In country after country, the statistics are staggering. Consider Tanzania: It takes an average of 379 days to start up a business. Moreover, it costs an average of $5,506, a figure many, many times the per capita income of $275.[17]

Although the situation is far worse in many other countries, even Canadians suffer from excessive regulations. For example, Joel Wood (2012) explains that housing regulations in Vancouver—establishing "minimum parking requirements, minimum suite sizes, fire regulations, and accessibility

---

17 Globalization at the Crossroads (2014). *The Power of the Poor: Bureaucracy and Corruption*. Web page. <http://www.thepowerofthepoor.com/concepts/c7.php>, as of April 10, 2014.

standards"—can unnecessarily drive up the price of housing. Wood cites the empirical studies (based on large U.S. cities) demonstrating that zoning regulations can push final home prices well above actual construction costs.[18]

Naturally, the proponents of zoning laws and other regulations on businesses would respond that they protect workers and consumers from dangerous working conditions and defective products. Yet often their analyses overlook the basic economic principle that there's no free lunch. As the extreme cases in Peru and Tanzania demonstrate, whatever benefits may flow from particular regulations must be weighed against the cost in terms of lower output. Even something as apparently "obvious" as government safety restrictions on the introduction of new drugs for medical treatment have a built-in tradeoff, as Milton and Rose Friedman stressed in their book *Free to Choose*. If the government insists on a battery of tests and other regulatory hurdles before allowing pharmaceutical companies to bring a new heart medication to market, that may indeed reduce the number of people who die from the side effects of an unsafe product. But on the other hand, the extra delay and expense may *also* mean that more people with heart conditions die, because the treatment is not yet available or is too expensive for them. What's worse, not only does this tradeoff exist, but government officials will have a natural tendency to err on the side of *denying* patients the option of trying new (and possibly risky) drugs or procedures, because it's much easier to point fingers at a government agency when someone dies from an unsafe product, rather than someone dying from a medical condition (but who would have survived had the government ruled differently). Once again, we see Bastiat's famous dichotomy between what is seen and unseen: When the government prohibits certain drugs and medical procedures, the public easily recognizes that this will reduce the damage resulting from defective products or unsafe procedures. Yet the people who would have been cured of their ailments had the government not prevented their access to effective treatments remain hidden.

In reality, the choice isn't between regulation and non-regulation, but rather between the *source* of regulations on business: voluntary, nuanced market processes with instant feedback, versus one-size-fits-all mandates issued

---

18 Joel Wood (2012). Free Our Cities. *Fraser Forum* (July/August). <http://www.fraserinstitute.org/uploadedFiles/fraser-ca/Content/research-news/research/articles/regulation-review-free-our-cities.pdf>, as of April 10, 2014.

from government bureaucracies. Consider, for example, a popular government regulation that economists have studied very carefully: rent control. This qualifies as a regulation because the government is dictating the terms on which landlords are legally allowed to rent their rooms to tenants; specifically, the government imposes a ceiling on rents, making it illegal to charge a higher price. As we discussed in Chapter One, rent control leads to many undesirable consequences, even from the point of view of the tenants. By short-circuiting the market process of "rationing" apartments through the price mechanism, rent control regulations lead to shortages, in which tenants want more apartments than landlords wish to rent. Rent control regulations also sabotage the normal working of competition, taking away landlords' incentives to respond quickly to tenant complaints. The market already has built-in channels through which the needs of tenants will be expressed, and the market provides landlords with the proper incentives to cater to them. The imposition of government rent control regulations doesn't merely add a layer of protection for tenants; instead it offers one benefit—lower rents—while stripping away other benefits. We see this pattern repeatedly when governments promulgate regulations on households and industry, where unintended consequences end up hurting even the alleged beneficiaries of the new rules.

One argument used to justify government—as opposed to market-based—regulations is that workers and consumers lack important information necessary to make qualified decisions. We can't rely on profit and loss signals, the critics claim, to ensure workplace safety and product purity, because it takes trained experts to identify risks. The average factory worker, for example, can't tell if a building is structurally sound, and the average consumer can't tell if a bottle of aspirin is poisonous.

It is true that workers and consumers lack the information *directly* to make all of the relevant decisions, but even so this observation is not a blank check for open-ended government regulations. There are many ways that genuine experts can communicate information through *market* processes. For example, large retail outlets such as Walmart or Target can employ experts to ensure that the lamps they import from China won't electrocute their customers, or that the handling procedures in their meat department will minimize the chance of food poisoning. Private trade associations can only allow qualified and reputable carpenters, plumbers, electricians, and other professionals to enter their ranks (in exchange for membership dues), providing information for consumers before they hire someone for work on their homes. There are organizations such as *Consumer Reports* and Underwriters Laboratories (with the familiar "UL" branding) that provide third-party testing and feedback for businesses and consumers alike. Large institutions, such as schools and hospitals, rely on experts and objective procedures before adding someone to their staff, because it would be very bad for business if, say, the math teacher didn't know algebra, or the brain surgeon had flunked out of medical school.

Thus, we see that there are numerous ways in which voluntary market forces can "regulate" businesses in order to protect both workers and consumers, which ultimately rely on the effects on reputation and future profitability. Beyond these mechanisms emanating purely from the market, there are also ex post legal remedies relying on the courts. For example, if someone *were* electrocuted by a lamp during routine use, his family would be able to sue the retailer and/or the manufacturer for damages. This is yet another reason that businesses have incentives *not* to sell dangerous products.[19]

Notice that what we mean by "government regulations" can often go above and beyond these safeguards, and *preemptively* tell businesses and households how they must behave. Prescriptive regulations may seem wise—with a little prevention being cheaper than dealing with a problem after it occurs—but we must keep in mind all of the ways government regulation can fail. For example, in early 2013 the federal government launched an investigation into the largest beef recall in Canadian history the year before (because of an E. coli outbreak). One media report said the "review is to focus on what contributed to the outbreak of the potentially deadly bacteria at the XL Foods Inc. plant in Brooks, Alta" but the Ottawa investigation "will also look at how well the Canadian Food Inspection Agency performed, including why tainted meat was distributed to retailers and sold to consumers."[20] Whenever a private business ends up hurting workers or consumers, the public's natural reaction is to blame "capitalism" and call for more stringent government regulations. Yet ironically, in First World countries today, whenever a problem occurs it is *amidst* government regulations that failed to do their job. Whether the

---

19 Of course, as our discussion of the notorious McDonald's coffee case shows, the threat of lawsuits will only lead to economically efficient behaviour if the awards are appropriate.

20 CBC News (2013, February 9). *Ottawa Launches Review into XL Foods E. Coli Outbreak.* Canadian Press. <http://www.cbc.ca/news/canada/story/2013/02/08/canada-xl-foods-beef-recall-cfia-agriculture. html> as of April 10, 2014.

solution is to give such agencies even more authority, or less, is an open question. What's telling here is that many people adopt the unreasonable attitude that government regulations can only help—and that the answer to government regulatory failure is more government regulation. An open-minded person should consider the possibility that moving in the *other* direction on the regulatory spectrum would yield a better outcome.

Another major drawback with explicit government regulation is what is termed "regulatory capture," in which the very government agencies supposedly acting as watch dogs are themselves populated with officials who are sympathetic to the industry they are policing. A perverse "revolving door" between industry and government can emerge, in which the top regulators of pharmaceutical companies or hedge funds know that they have a whole career of lucrative consulting and advisory positions waiting for them once they leave public service, so long as they "play ball" while making key decisions affecting these important firms.

One particularly insidious aspect of regulatory capture occurs when powerful firms with a large share of the market paradoxically support new, sweeping regulations on their industry, because they perceive that these regulations will be costlier on smaller competitors. For example, large corporations have entire accounting departments, and can more easily comply with new regulations that require mounds of paperwork. Thus, large corporations can sometimes cast themselves as the "good guys" who publicly (and behind-the-scenes) support a new regulation, *not* because they actually care about serving the public interest, but because they know full well it will harm their smaller rivals relatively more.[21]

The empirical literature confirms these warnings. For example, Feldmann (2009b) uses data from 19 industrial countries for five years in the period from 1990 to 2002. His regression analysis indicates that business regulations such as price controls, as well as administrative hurdles in opening

---

21 Economists use the term "Baptists and Bootleggers" to explain the phenomenon by which apparently opposed groups can embrace the same government regulation. In the historical example that gave rise to the term, in the United States both religious preachers (Baptists) and organized crime (bootleggers) supported the prohibition of alcohol. The Baptists supported the measure because of their moral and religious convictions, while the bootleggers supported it because they derived their income from selling alcohol on the black market. Economist Bruce Yandle coined the term originally.

new businesses, reduce labour force participation and employment rates, with substantial impacts on the low-skilled. In a separate paper, Feldmann (2009c) looks specifically at regulations on labour—such as restrictions on hiring and firing decisions—across 73 different countries from 2000 to 2003. Horst finds that tighter labour market regulations lead to substantially higher rates of unemployment, especially among young people.

If governments are going to regulate to attempt to improve on a private enterprise outcome, they should ensure that regulations are as effective (i.e. they actually resolve the perceived problem) and efficient (i.e. they minimize costs) as possible. To that end, governments should implement regulations that are performance (or outcome)-based rather than prescriptive. Prescriptive regulation forces individuals and/or organizations to behave in a very specific manner. That is, they detail how organizations must comply with regulations. In comparison, performance (or outcome)-based regulation sets a desired outcome that individuals and/or organizations must meet. With performance-based regulations, organizations are free to determine how to achieve the desired results. This provides them with significantly more flexibility, encourages innovation and ultimately reduces the costs imposed by the regulation.

Because there are always tradeoffs, prescriptive and excessive government restrictions on business can stifle entrepreneurship and raise consumer prices. Government regulations can displace more effective "private" regulatory mechanisms, and in perverse situations can actually lead large companies to use regulatory rules to shield themselves from competition. Economic prosperity thus depends on limited and outcome-based regulations.

Institutional Prerequisite #3

Competitive markets

One of the most important institutions for a prosperous economy is competitive markets. The phrase itself, competitive markets, has become quite maligned since the financial crisis of 2008. Indeed, many people have simply forgotten what a competitive market actually means. Simply put, markets are based on voluntary exchange between willing sellers and buyers. In addition, individuals and firms should be fairly free to enter and exit markets as opportunities arise. Free and open competition in labour and product markets allows workers and consumers to enjoy the benefits of capitalism that we have been discussing.

Without competition for labour, workers would be in dire straits. They would be at the complete mercy of employers, because most people need an outside paycheck in order to survive. Yet with competitive labour markets, there are many potential employers from which individuals can choose. If a particular job is too stressful, or a particular boss is abusive, the employee has the legal right to quit, and can seek alternate sources of income.

Not only do competitive labour markets give workers an ultimate "exit option," they also produce a tendency for workers to be paid fairly for their contribution to the company's bottom line, in accordance with what economists call their *marginal productivity*. For example, suppose that a particular worker raises his firm's total profits (not including the worker's paycheck) by $60,000, but the worker only receives $40,000 in salary. Although such an outcome is certainly *possible* in a market economy, there is an automatic incentive for a rival employer to offer the same worker a comparable position that pays, say, $50,000. This would represent a huge raise to the worker, justifying the hassle of interviewing and switching companies, but it would also reap the new company a net gain of $10,000 per year, justifying the costs of "headhunting" for such opportunities.

In the real world, there are many frictions and complications to this simple tale, but its essence remains correct: Competitive labour markets provide an incentive for companies to make job offers to workers who are currently *under*paid by the present employer. Especially as technology advances, there are growing opportunities for compatible workers and employers to "find" each other, improving wages and profits respectively. There are established "temp" and long-term job placement agencies that specialize in facilitating such match-ups, and with the Internet the costs of job search have fallen dramatically.

Competitive markets also protect consumers from high prices and inferior products. Yes, there may be regulations in place—both formal ones issued by the government and informal ones supported by market practices—but the *ultimate* check on consumer abuse is the ability to "vote with one's dollars" by switching to another seller. In a competitive market, a producer must constantly strive for customer satisfaction, finding ways to improve product quality and service, while watching costs to maintain affordable prices.

Just as competition pushes wage rates to reflect a worker's productivity, it also provides a tendency for consumer prices to reflect the actual costs of production. For example, if a retail outlet can import television sets for $20 and then sell them for $250, that is a gigantic markup that provides a huge profit opportunity for a competitor to enter the scene, offering the same product for $200 and capturing a large portion of the original store's customers.

To be sure, in the real world, retailers would never want to whittle away the mark-up to *zero*, as this would eliminate their own motivation to stay in business. Additionally, there are cases where at first glance it *seems* there is a persistent and unfair mark-up, when in reality the seller is creating a unique product that consumers value more than the original materials. Good examples of this would be Nike running shoes or Bauer hockey skates. Here again, so long as there is competition, where consumers are free to patronize *generic* producers of comparable items, then the market is performing well: People can splurge if they want to enjoy the prestige of owning the name-brand items, or they can pay much lower prices if they don't care about such matters.

Related to the importance of competitive markets is the social function of advertising. To many critics, advertising epitomizes the worst features of a market economy, as it often relies on low-brow humor, emotional appeals, and over-the-top claims. Nonetheless, the reality of our world is that *information is scarce*, and advertising (both in labour and product markets) is vital to ensure healthy competition. After all, it does a consumer little good if a rival store is offering the same television set for $50 less, if the consumer never learns of the deal. Furthermore, marketing campaigns are designed the way they are, because they *work*. For whatever reason, people often respond to emotional appeals rather than intellectual arguments, and they may patronize a certain brand because they remember a catchy jingle. Marketing campaigns merely reflect how real people respond. The elites who disdain commercial culture really have a problem with humanity, not with advertisers per se.

Although government officials will often warn against "monopolistic" private businesses, ironically the government itself often restricts competition. For example, Toronto—like other major cities—restricts the number of taxis by issuing a limited number of licenses giving permission to operate a cab. Although other drivers appreciate the limitation of cabs on the road, the downside is a restriction in supply and hence higher fare prices for consumers. To get a sense of just how serious the restriction is, consider that in 2013, a standard Toronto taxi license could be sold to another operator for up to $400,000.[22]

Government-imposed caps on taxi operators are a specific example of *occupational licensing*, which harks back to feudal times when people needed to join a guild before being allowed to practice a certain craft. It is understandable—though still a restriction on competition—when the government insists on numerous educational and testing milestones before granting a license to practice law or medicine. Yet in practice, governments have placed arbitrary limits on the people allowed to braid hair. Such absurdities aren't just humorous; they restrict supply, which definitely means higher prices for consumers and possibly lower quality as well, as the normal competitive mechanism is crippled. Beyond the harm to consumers, such entry-level restrictions also make it difficult for poor individuals, with little formal education, to lift themselves out of poverty.

In a 2008 paper, Gerry Angevine and Jerry Thomson argued that "[p]rovincial licensing and certification requirements, federal employment insurance rules, and the lack of reciprocal agreements with other countries constrain skilled workers from entering the Alberta workforce."[23] They recommended liberalization of the barriers to worker mobility, which would allow for faster job

---

22 Jessica Smith (2013, March 11). Getting a Fare Deal: Why Toronto's Taxi Industry is Failing, and What to Do about It. *Metro Toronto*. <http://metronews.ca/news/toronto/589821/why-torontos-taxi-industry-is-failing-and-what-to-do-about-it/>, as of April 10, 2014.

23 Gerry Angevine and Graham Thomson (2008). *Eliminating Barriers to Worker Mobility: Increasing the Availability of Skilled Labor in Alberta's Oil Sands Industry.* Fraser Alert (July).

growth and economic development in Alberta, but would also improve labour conditions for workers in other provinces and even other countries.

Empirical studies show the benefits of competitive markets, even beyond mere pecuniary outcomes. For example, de Soysa and Vadlammanati (2011) analyze data from 117 countries over the period 1981 to 2006, and find that reforms leading to more competitive markets are associated with fewer human rights violations.

Competitive markets are a crucial ingredient to economic prosperity. The government must refrain from placing arbitrary restrictions on businesses and workers.

Institutional Prerequisite #4

An efficient financial market

In Chapter One we stressed the importance of saving to a country's long-run growth. But a country needs an efficient financial market in order to *channel* its savings into wise investments. By "financial market" we broadly refer to commercial banks and credit unions, but also the stock and bond markets, and even insurance companies. There are myriad routes in the modern Canadian economy through which savers can lend or invest their funds. It is crucial for economic progress that this market for financial flows runs smoothly.

To understand why, first let's consider the benefits of *financial intermediation*, which means the process of a "middleman" connecting savers with borrowers. For example, consider a local bank issuing a home mortgage of $200,000, with a 6% interest rate, to a young couple. Even though the bank is making the loan, it obtained the money (let us suppose) from 200 of the couple's neighbours, who each deposited $1,000 into the same bank in their savings accounts, which earn 2% interest. Why, if the couple is ultimately borrowing the savings provided by their neighbours, do they bother with the bank at all? Why doesn't the couple borrow $1,000 from each of their 200 neighbors, at a rate of 4%—thus cutting out the middleman, and benefiting everyone involved?

The answer is obvious upon a moment's reflection. For one thing, it would be cumbersome for the couple to carry out negotiations with 200

*Hi, we're trying to buy a house
and wondered if you'd like to
lend us $50 at 3% for 30 years?*

separate people. Yet more fundamental, it would be very *risky* for the neighbors to lend their savings to the couple; a simple layoff or sickness might mean a default on the "mortgage" (owed directly to the neighbours). By working through the bank—which takes in deposits from many thousands of individuals and has a portfolio consisting of hundreds of mortgages—the risk is spread out. Assuming the bank's loan officers do a good job in assessing default rates and charge higher interest rates accordingly, the depositors can enjoy a lower—but more certain—return on their savings. The "spread" between the interest rate that the bank charges and what it pays constitutes the source of the bank's income, out of which it pays its loan officers and other expenses. A profitable, stable bank is one that channels its depositors' funds into those projects—such as homes and commercial real estate—with appropriate risk/reward attributes.

Yet commercial banks are not the only mechanism in a modern economy through which savings are channeled into investments. In the bond market, for example, corporations and governments issue IOUs (legally binding promises to pay a sum of money later) in exchange for money upfront. A corporation might borrow $1,000 from 1,000 separate lenders, issuing them each a one-year bond promising to pay back $1,050. If the corporation invests the $1 million wisely, it will earn more than enough over the course of the year in order to repay its lenders plus interest. Corporations that are considered riskier will need to offer higher yields on their bonds, in order to attract lenders.

There is nothing wrong with people investing in risky bonds, so long as they *understand* the risks; after all, we wouldn't want *all* of a nation's investments devoted merely to "sure things," as this would stifle innovation. In an efficient financial market, ratings agencies provide accurate information about the likelihood of default on bonds issued by various corporations, so that investors can accurately gauge the relative risk/reward involved. Just as consumer preferences dictate the colour and sizes of clothing produced in a market economy, so too do investor preferences guide the types of investments that are made.

Another common mechanism for channeling saving is the stock market. When a corporation issues new shares of stock, it takes in money from investors who then become partial owners of the corporation itself. In an efficient financial market, the prices of various stocks will tend to reflect the future profitability of the firms in question. For newly issued shares of stock, an accurate price is important because it channels a greater volume of savings—because of the higher stock price—to those firms that are expected to produce the most with their investments.

Even in the secondary market, where individuals buy and sell existing shares of stock, it is important for the price to reflect the underlying "fundamentals" of the company. To take an extreme example, suppose the shares of Suncor Energy suddenly traded at a fraction of a penny (instead of $31, as of this writing). At this low price, an eccentric investor could plunk down $1 million to buy a majority stake in the giant company, and proceed on a harebrained scheme to relocate all company resources into drilling for oil at the North Pole. Recall from Chapter One that market prices for labour and other resources help ensure that they are channeled into those lines where they are needed most; the high price of gold, for example, prevents it from being squandered in an ostentatious coating of apartment units. By the same token, the high share price of Suncor helps ensure that its massive holdings of sophisticated equipment, infrastructure, and "human capital" are deployed effectively.

The more sophisticated derivatives market also serves a useful social function, by helping to allocate risk among the parties most willing to bear it. For example, the owner of an oil well might sell *futures contracts* on crude oil, while an airline might buy them. In this way, the two parties effectively lock in the price at which they will sell and buy crude oil in the future. By hedging themselves against future volatility in oil prices, both parties will be more comfortable in expanding their operations: the well owner is protected against a sharp drop in oil prices, while the airline is protected against a sharp rise in fuel costs. The availability of a futures market in oil allows the two to "split the difference" and invest with confidence.

There are many examples of government interventions that undermine the efficiency of the financial market, and thereby retard economic growth. For example, during the early years of the Great Depression the United States suffered thousands of bank failures, while Canada was relatively unscathed. Milton Friedman and Anna Schwartz explained this discrepancy by the prevalence of "unit banking" regulations in the U.S., in which states prohibited branch banking. The branches of Canadian banks in hard-hit regions were able to weather the storm, because they were part of a nationwide network. In contrast, a bank confined to a particular state such as Idaho was devastated when collapsing wheat prices meant that farmers defaulted on their loans in droves.[24]

Another government distortion of the financial market is the encouragement of debt financing versus equity financing. Consider: if a corporation raises $1 million to fund a new factory by issuing 10-year bonds, then the interest it pays reduces its net income, thus lowering its corporate tax liability. On the other hand, if the corporation raises the same $1 million by issuing new shares of stock—and then rewarding the investors by paying dividends over the next decade—these dividend payments would *not* be a deductible expense, but instead would be classified as distributing the profits back to the

---

24 See Jim Powell (2003). *FDR's Folly: How Roosevelt and His New Deal Prolonged the Great Depression.* Three Rivers Press: 32.

owners. Thus, when critics of capitalism wonder why firms take on so much debt and become dangerously "leveraged," one answer is that the tax code implicitly pays them to do so.

In the wake of the financial crisis of 2008, governments and central banks around the world engaged in unprecedented programs to "bail out" investment banks and other institutions that had made reckless investment decisions during the housing bubble years. Although such programs were hailed as necessary to prevent an outright collapse, nonetheless they corroded the efficient functioning of the financial markets. Capitalism is a profit *and loss* system. Regrettably, the lesson from this episode was that firms should take on great risk during boom times, reaping the lucrative profits as the markets soar upward. Then, in the collapse, the losses of these reckless firms will be "socialized" onto the backs of the taxpayers and everyone holding dollar-denominated assets. Financial institutions will only responsibly allocate capital—having the farsightedness to eschew high rewards when the risk is too great—if they are made to bear the brunt of their losses, should they occur.

More generally, government guarantees of commercial bank deposits also create what economists call "moral hazard" and serve to undermine a healthy financial market. Because they are made whole in the event of a bank collapse, depositors have no incentive to perform due diligence when selecting a bank. Customers will tend to place their money with whatever bank offers the highest interest rate, regardless of the riskiness of the loans it makes. Thus, government guarantees on depository institutions, though preventing "bank runs," weaken competition among banks and place the burden of risk oversight on government regulators.

Finally, even laws and regulations restricting "insider trading" and "corporate raiders" can actually reduce the efficiency of the financial market. If an "insider" knows that, say, a pending lawsuit will cause a stock to plummet, then his rush to "short" the stock communicates vital information to everyone else. The stock price begins to fall sooner than the actual announcement of the verdict, making the swings in its price less volatile than they would be without the action of the insider. Regarding corporate raiders, they can only earn a profit if management is so poorly running a company that its assets are worth more being sold off to the highest bidders. In such a scenario, the corporate raiders are actually the friends of the stockholders, who are being underserved by the existing management. The threat of a "hostile takeover" actually serves as a check on corporate bureaucracy, and can ultimately redistribute resources to other firms when they are not being efficiently used in a particular enterprise.

There are empirical studies to back up our above arguments. For example, James Lothian (2006) investigates the puzzle of why more capital doesn't flow from rich to poor countries (where it would presumably earn a higher rate of return on the margin). He finds that the underlying institutional structures are important; countries with policies that promote price stability and that have fewer direct government interventions are associated with higher capital inflows.

For another example, Sinclair Davidson (2005) analyzed the 1997-98 Asian financial crisis using stock market returns, and found that the countries with "pegged and managed exchange rate regimes performed worse than those with floating exchange rate regimes." In other words, Davidson found that countries with governments that interfered in currency markets to (allegedly) prevent "unfair" speculative attacks and other problems ended up suffering more when the financial crisis struck.

Roychoudhury and Lawson (2010) use regression analysis and find that (after controlling for obvious factors such as per capita production) a 2.4 standard deviation drop in the Fraser Institute's Economic Freedom Index led to approximately a 50% higher borrowing cost for the government. In other words, the market for sovereign debt viewed governments that provided less economic freedom as more likely to default on their bonds.

Hall, Sobel, and Crowley (2010) reverse the argument, and use cross-country growth regressions to argue that those countries with "good" institutions experience output growth in response to increases in human and physical capital. However, they find that countries with "bad" institutions actually see a reduction in growth when capital increases, because the new capital tends to be employed in unproductive "rent-seeking" activities. In a similar paper, Gwartney, Holcombe, and Lawson (2006) look at data from 94 countries during the period 1980 to 2000. They conclude that countries with high scores on the Fraser Institute's Economic Freedom Index not only have higher levels of investment, but that the *productivity* of private investment was 74% higher.

Saving and investment are necessary for long-run economic growth. An efficient financial market is the crucial institutional prerequisite to ensure that savings are properly channeled into the correct investment outlets.

Institutional Prerequisite #5

Sound money

Economists formally define *money* as a "medium of exchange" that is commonly accepted. In plain English, this means that all of the people in a society are willing to trade away their goods and services in exchange for a single commodity, which they desire *not* for its own sake, but because they intend to trade it away again in the future. Such a commodity is the *money* in this society. By *sound* money, we mean money that has a predictable value over time, not subject to sudden fluctuations in its purchasing power.

To understand the importance of sound money, we should try to imagine an economy *without* money. In such a world, there would be a much smaller scope for trade, which in turn would mean that people couldn't afford to specialize in various occupations. For example, it wouldn't make sense for a man to go through the education and training to become a dentist, because whenever he wanted to eat a steak, he'd have to find a butcher with a toothache. (Economists refer to this as the problem of a "double coincidence of wants.") This inconvenience is solved with a generally accepted medium of exchange— i.e., money—because it allows a person to sell items or services to a buyer

Er, I don't really need a watch. Have you got anything else I might need?

for money, and then use the money to buy desired items or services from somebody else. The use of money therefore facilitates far more complex trading patterns than would be possible under barter. Because sale and purchase have effectively been separated into two transactions, money allows people to specialize in occupations where they have an advantage.

Besides encouraging specialization, the institution of money also fosters long-term planning. In principle, we could imagine people making retirement plans in terms of extensive contracts that did not mention money at all. For example, a schoolteacher could give reading and arithmetic lessons to her young students, in exchange for them agreeing to mow her lawn, bring her groceries, and vacuum her house when she is in her 70s. But to even imagine such a scenario shows how farfetched and cumbersome it would be. The existence of money allows the schoolteacher to teach her students in exchange for money (paid by their parents, presumably), which she can then either hold or invest in other assets that will (she hopes) return a greater amount of money in the future, when she is no longer working yet still wants to have her lawn cut, buy groceries, etc.

Another indispensable function of money is that it makes calculations of profit and loss possible, by reducing every item in the market to a common denominator. Imagine looking at a complex business enterprise, where, say, the entrepreneur hired a group of workers to use steel, electricity, rubber, glass, and other inputs in order to produce a batch of motorcycles. Was this a wise use of scarce resources or was it wasteful? Without market prices for the items involved, this question would be impossible to answer, because there is no principle in engineering or chemistry to explain the "socially advantageous" relations between these inputs and the output of the motorcycles. Yet with money (and competitive markets for the various goods), it is a simple matter for an accountant to tell the entrepreneur whether the operation is in the black or the red. In Chapter One we explained how profits (and losses) helped guide entrepreneurs to steer resources into the proper channels. Those profits and losses can only be recognized in a community using money.

Economists have long recognized that with money, what is true for the individual is not true for society as a whole. Any particular person obviously benefits if he acquires more money. For example, a man would be delighted to wake up one morning, only to discover that the $100 in his wallet had magically doubled to $200; he would be able to go out into the market and buy more physical goods than the day before. Yet if *everyone* woke up to find a doubled stock of money, on average they would be no richer than before. Simply doubling the number of pieces of paper wouldn't create more televisions, sushi dinners, bicycles, or farmland. In "real" terms, the community would be just as wealthy as it was the day before. As people tried to spend their new-found money, they would push up the prices on this same collection of goods and services. Depending on the specifics, some people might benefit (because they spent their new money on items before the price had adequately risen), but only at the expense of other people who would lose. Most economists agree that in the long run, increases in the stock of money do not increase the output of real goods and services, but merely increase their unit prices.

Even though the community as a whole is not made richer by printing new money, the organization in charge of the printing press certainly is. (Ask yourself: Moral issues aside, would it be fun to have the ability to print off crisp new $100 bills in your home office?) Throughout history, governments have succumbed to this temptation, often to the point of disaster. The most famous example is the interwar Weimar Republic, in which the German authorities so debased their currency that wives had to go to their husbands' places of work to receive the pay and rush to market to spend it on anything, while restaurant diners would insist on paying when they first sat down to avoid the price inflation during the meal. More recently, Zimbabwe destroyed its currency through reckless printing, with the measured rate of annual price inflation exceeding an astonishing *89 sextillion percent* (that's 10^{21}).[25]

Fortunately, Canadians have never had to endure such extremes, but they, too, suffered through high and volatile rates of inflation throughout the 1970s and 1980s, as **Figure 2.1** indicates.

When the future purchasing power of money is rendered uncertain by government policy, it partially defeats the advantages of having money in the first place. Households and firms have difficulty making long-term financial plans, because they are reluctant to commit to decisions (such as taking out a mortgage or issuing a bond) that are specified in dollar amounts. When making investment decisions, people in an inflationary environment are pushed into "hedges" such as gold and silver, and no longer place as much emphasis

---

25 The Cato Institute's Steve Hanke has a page devoted to the Zimbabwe disaster at <http://www.cato.org/zimbabwe>, as of April 15, 2014.

Figure 2.1: Annual inflation rates in Canada, 1915–2013

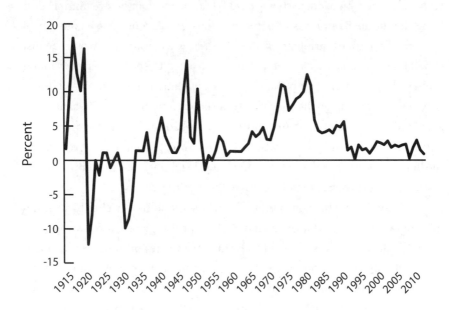

Source: Statistics Canada, CANSIM Table 326-0021.

on the other attributes of various assets; the primary consideration is, "How will this asset fare, if prices in general keep rising at a rapid rate?"

Another perverse effect is that business owners might be fooled by phantom profits during an inflationary boom. Because of the influx of new money, their customers are able to bid up prices, leading the owners to believe they are doing quite well. Yet if they do not correctly anticipate the increase in their own costs—such as replacing worn out equipment—they may unwittingly "eat the seedcorn" of their operations by failing to reinvest enough out of their surge in revenues.[26]

For all of these reasons, sound money is essential for economic prosperity. As Vladimir Lenin reputedly said, the best way to destroy capitalism is to debauch the currency. The peer-reviewed empirical literature confirms these (obvious) lessons of history. For example, Bjornskov and Foss (2008) looked at the individual components of the Fraser Institute's Economic

---

26 For a scholarly yet accessible explanation of the "microeconomic" problems with large inflation, see Horwitz (2003).

Freedom Index to see which were correlated with entrepreneurship data from the Global Entrepreneurship Monitor. They found that the size of government had a negative correlation, while the "sound money" measure had a positive correlation—meaning it increased entrepreneurship. In contrast, the other measures of economic freedom had no significant effect on entrepreneurship one way or the other.

Institutional Prerequisite #6

Low, uniform tax rates

With government spending comes the inevitability of government taxation to finance it. The more the government spends (and taxes), the fewer resources that will be available for private consumption and investment. Moreover, once the citizens agree on the level of government spending they desire, the *method* the government uses to raise the necessary revenue is still vitally important. In short, not all tax codes are created equal. Different ways of trying to raise a given amount of revenue will have different effects on growth and prosperity. Through both theory and observation, economists know that the *structure* of taxation is as important as the *level* of taxation.

As we discussed in Chapter One, people respond to incentives and make decisions on the margin. Because of this, high *marginal* tax rates can be particularly damaging to economic efficiency and growth. (The marginal tax rate refers to how much the government takes of an *additional* pre-tax dollar that the taxpayer obtains.) The beneficial mechanisms of private enterprise that we have discussed—its tendency to facilitate mutually advantageous trades and to steer resources to their best uses—are hampered when high taxes distort price signals.

When the government places a tax on a particular good, it raises its price and alters people's decisions, even though the underlying "fundamentals" haven't changed. For example, if the government imposes a tax on alcoholic beverages but not on bottled water, this makes the alcohol artificially expensive and causes people to shift their purchases. (Indeed, for many proponents of a tax on alcohol, that's the *point*—to reduce consumption.) The same principle operates if the government taxes income: It artificially reduces the rewards from earning extra income and therefore lowers the lower the incentives for individuals to work hard, invest and engage in entrepreneurship.

Some critics downplay the notion that high marginal income tax rates would discourage work effort, because (they claim) people will always choose the occupation in which they earn the most, based on an after-tax analysis. Yet this is a very naïve view that overlooks the subtleties of the real world. For example, suppose a stay-at-home wife is considering taking an office job that would pay (before taxes) $500 per week in wages. However, when discussing this option, she and her husband are realistic, and know that the extra dry cleaning for her work attire, and the higher food budget if she has to eat lunch at work and is no longer able to prepare dinner every night, will mean that the household spends an extra $125 per week if she takes the job. In the absence of tax considerations, the couple might decide that the net gain of $375 per week is worth her having to get up at 6 a.m. and go deal with a boss five days a week. But if the couple faces a marginal tax rate of 30% out of the wife's gross $500 paycheck, the couple will only retain $350, which will be further reduced to $225 because of the extra dry cleaning and takeout from restaurants. Although the couple would still have a higher income if the wife takes the job, the net gain of a mere $225 per week might not be worth the hassle. The economy would then lose out on the wife's potential output in the office because of the tax code, even though her employer would be willing to pay her enough to make it worth her while to produce it.

For another example, consider a man with a $100,000 salary working for an engineering firm in the suburbs of Ottawa. He gets an offer for a $150,000 job at a company located downtown. The money is attractive, but the downsides of the job are that it would be a more stressful work environment, and the man would have to spend an extra 90 minutes per day commuting to and from the city. Suppose that if there were no tax considerations, the man would take job; this would be an efficient use of resources, as the higher productivity of his output in the downtown firm would be enough to compensate him for the stress and longer commute. Yet if he faces a marginal tax rate of 40%, then of his $50,000 pay raise, the man would actually only get to keep $30,000 in extra take-home pay. For what is effectively a $30,000 pay hike, it might not be worth it for the man to switch jobs, and thus the economy loses out on his (potential) higher output at the downtown firm.

High marginal tax rates reduce work effort even in cases where it would seem they should have no impact. For example, most people would assume that a star athlete would not change career paths because of tax considerations; a young man who is drafted by a professional hockey team will presumably jump at the opportunity, regardless of tax brackets, rather than taking a more mundane position. However, how long a star athlete such as Wayne Gretzky *postpones retirement* is certainly something that could be affected by the tax code. For another example, how often a famous rock band goes on tour could be affected by tax considerations. Of course people with the necessary talent and dedication will become superstar musicians, rather than librarians, whether the top marginal income tax rate is 10% or 50%. But once they've made it and are already rich and famous, an established group might only go on, say, three world tours, rather than eight, if the government takes half of their earnings as opposed to only a tenth. The Beatles even wrote a song about the "Taxman" referring to the U.K's outrageous 95% "super-tax" of the time ("There's one for you / nineteen for me").[27]

High tax rates distort business decisions as well. For example, if the tax code allows firms to provide certain benefits (such as use of a company car, cell phone, and computer, or access to company dental benefits) without forcing the employees to recognize them as in-kind income on their personal taxes, then firms will end up offering compensation packages that don't really line up with employee preferences. Suppose a firm could offer an employee either $100,000 in salary, or $70,000 in salary and use of a $20,000 car. In the absence of tax considerations, the employee would clearly prefer the first option, as the employee could go buy the car himself, and still have an extra $10,000. Yet if the employee faces a marginal tax rate of 50%, *and* the tax code doesn't recognize the use of the company car as a taxable benefit, then the employee might prefer the second compensation package, because it effectively delivers him use of a $20,000 car with only a reduction of $15,000 in after-tax salary. Yet clearly, this is an inefficient decision considering the fundamentals; the employee perversely prefers a compensation package worth $90,000 to one worth $100,000.

High taxes levied on business income also induce inefficiently exorbitant purchases, because they obscure the true economic cost of the choices.

---

27 See <http://www.thebeatles.com/song/taxman> as of April 15, 2014.

For example, suppose that a business owner is in the market to lease a vehicle to be used for business. He has narrowed his choices to a sedan that carries an annual lease of $200 per month that would satisfy his needs, versus a much nicer SUV that would cost $450 per month. In the absence of tax considerations, suppose that the man would go for the cheaper vehicle, because he has better ways of spending the extra $250 per month that the SUV would require. However, if the man faces a 50% marginal income tax rate, then the amount he spends on leasing a new vehicle is a business expense and hence a significant tax write-off. Leasing the sedan really only costs him $100 per month in after-tax income, and the SUV really only costs him $225 per month. Thus, the difference between the two has *also* been cut in half; the man might decide that on the margin, he would rather drive the SUV around town than have an extra $125 (the difference between $225 and $100) in after-tax income to spend on other goods and services each month. In this example, the tax code has induced him to lease a nicer vehicle for his business than he really should have; the market's normal penalties on extravagant spending are muted by the tax on business income.

Economists stress yet another distortion that comes from taxing interest and dividend income: It reduces the incentive to save and hence lowers investment and long-run economic growth. Suppose the return on an equity mutual fund (meaning a fund that holds stocks) averages 10% per year. In the absence of tax considerations, that means a person who has $1,000 to work with can either spend it now, on current enjoyments, or he can invest it and have access to $1,100 next year. Based on this tradeoff, the person will decide how much he wants to save. Yet if the interest and dividend income, or "realized capital gains," are taxed at, say, 15%, then the man faces a choice between enjoying $1,000 in present consumption versus $1,085 available next year. Clearly the incentive for saving has been reduced, which (other things equal) will lead citizens to save and invest less than they otherwise would have. Note that this effect is *on top* of the disincentive to work, emanating from a tax on wage income: Even after a worker has paid the taxes on his base salary, his decision on whether to spend those after-tax wages on present versus future enjoyments is again distorted if the government taxes interest, dividends, and capital gains.

In light of these considerations, many economists think the ideal tax code is one that allows the government to run a balanced budget (on average) with a low, *flat* rate applied to as broad a base of taxpayers as possible. Giving special deductions and exemptions to certain goods or activities reduces the distortions in those sectors, it is true, but for a fixed target of revenue desired, "loopholes" in some sectors imply higher tax rates in others. By making the underlying tax base as broad as possible, the single marginal tax rate applied to it can be minimized, reducing the overall distortions and denying the government the temptation to pick "winners and losers" through preferential tax treatment.[28] Furthermore, many economists argue that tax reform should replace income taxes (especially on interest, dividends, and capital gains) with consumption-based taxes, to remove the artificial penalty on saving.

There should be no illusion that an "ideal" tax code is possible: If the government takes resources from the private sector, it will distort decisions and cause inefficiencies (which in theory might be compensated by wise government spending of the revenue). Even a low, flat tax on consumption will ultimately reduce the rewards from working, saving, and investing, meaning a country's private sector output and growth will be lower (relative to a

---

28 It is important to limit the discretionary power government officials have in picking "winners and losers" for at least two reasons. First, there is no reason to expect these officials to have more wisdom than the decentralized market, which can draw on the dispersed knowledge of (potentially) millions of people. Second, if the government doles out favours (and punishments) somewhat arbitrarily, it gives an incentive for special interest groups to devote resources to currying favour with the relevant decision-makers. Economists call this rent seeking, and view it as a waste of resources from a social perspective.

completely tax-free scenario). Yet the important point is that some tax codes impose far worse distortions than others, even for the same level of revenue extraction.

A plethora of scholarly studies confirms these results. For example, Engen and Skinner (1996) surveyed more than 20 papers from the peer-reviewed literature and concluded that "a major tax reform reducing all marginal rates by five percentage points… is predicted to increase long-term growth rates by between 0.2 and 0.3 percentage points." Young Lee and Roger Gordon (2005) looked at data for 70 countries for the period from 1970 to 1997, and found that a reduction of ten percentage points in corporate tax rates raised a country's growth rate by one to two percentage points. Bergh and Karlsson (2010) examined a sample of wealthy countries from 1970 to 2005, and found that the size of government—measured by tax receipts and spending relative to GDP—is negatively associated with economic growth.

One of the most carefully designed studies—published in the prestigious *American Economic Review*—comes from former Obama administration Chair of the Council of Economic Advisers Christina Romer and co-author David Romer. In a 2010 paper that developed a new measure of fiscal shocks, the Romers classified every major tax-change episode from the U.S. postwar period and concluded that "an exogenous tax increase of 1% of GDP lowers real GDP by roughly 3%" (Romer and Romer 2010).

Both economic theory and empirical study suggest that low, uniform tax rates are essential for economic prosperity.

Institutional Prerequisite #7

Low trade barriers (free trade)

It has been said that the benefits of *free trade*—meaning that governments do not put up discriminatory tax or regulatory hurdles in the way of goods crossing over their national borders—is something on which virtually all economists agree, yet which is surprisingly difficult to teach to the general public. No matter how compelling the logic or statistics offered in support of free trade, the average person seems to instinctively endorse a proposal to "protect jobs here at home" by putting up barriers to keep "cheap imports" out of the country.

The prejudice in favour of *protectionism*—a term describing government policies that (allegedly) favour domestic job creation by reducing competition from foreign producers—is actually quite old. Centuries ago, this same mentality was embodied in *mercantilism*, the doctrine that a nation grew rich by acquiring precious metals. The mercantilists could see that an individual household grew wealthy by producing more than it consumed, and thus building up a balance of financial wealth. They applied that same reasoning to the country as a whole, and thought that the path to national riches was to have exports exceed imports—to run a "trade surplus"—so that more gold and silver flowed *into* the country (when foreigners bought its exports) than flowed *out* of the country (when domestic residents spent money on imports). Because of this mentality, the mercantilists favoured government policies that subsidized exports and penalized imports, to try to force a larger trade surplus than would otherwise have occurred.

There were many problems with mercantilist thinking. For one thing, it encouraged international conflict, because it relied on a "beggar thy neighbour" philosophy. Consider: If some countries were successful in their mercantilist agenda to have a growing trade surplus, then simple accounting required that other countries were *unsuccessful* and would have to show a growing trade *deficit*. (One nation's export is another nation's import; the world as a whole can't export more than it imports.) Mercantilism was based on "zero-sum game" thinking, where one nation's greatness depended on another nation's subservience. When major governments were animated by such (erroneous) economic doctrines, it led to unnecessary hostility between them.

The great achievement of the classical economists—including giants such as David Hume, Adam Smith, and David Ricardo—was to demolish the case for mercantilism. In contrast to the harsh view of the mercantilists, the classical economists showed that international trade was a *positive-sum* game, where all participants would benefit. (We have already seen how voluntary trade benefits both parties at the individual level; it works at the national level too, though it is a more involved process.) Indeed, the very title of Adam Smith's most famous book alludes to his insight that the wealth of nations does *not* consist of the accumulation of yellow or silver hunks of metal. Rather, the wealth of a nation consists in the flow of goods and services that its workers, equipment, and natural resources can produce. It was not the accumulation of money per se that signified true riches, but the standard of living enjoyed by a nation's members.

Once we shift the focus away from the accumulation of money, and look instead to all of the things that money can buy, the case for free trade becomes clear. As Smith wrote: "It is the maxim of every prudent master of a family, never to attempt to make at home what it will cost him more to make than to buy... What is prudence in the conduct of every private family, can scarce be folly in that of a great kingdom."[29]

In this famous quote, Smith argued that a nation becomes richer by importing those goods that other nations can produce more cheaply. Just as *individuals* do better by specializing in those niches in which they excel, and then trading their surplus production with each other, so too does a similar principle hold at the national level.

The logic of free trade is easy enough to grasp when we consider two countries where each has an *absolute advantage* in making their respective goods. For example, if we consider only Canada and the Bahamas, and focus just on crude oil and coconuts, it's very intuitive that the Canadians should devote themselves to extracting crude oil, while the Bahamians should devote themselves to harvesting coconuts. Then, after trading some coconuts for oil, the Canadians and Bahamians will have more of *both* goods than would be physically possible if each group had renounced the benefits of international trade. In this example, the reason is obvious: Canada has a huge natural advantage in producing crude oil, while the Bahamas has a huge natural advantage

---

29 Smith, Book IV, Chapter 2.

in producing coconuts. Just as a farmer and a tailor can obviously benefit by swapping food for clothes, so too are there obvious gains from trade between Canada and the Bahamas if they swap oil for coconuts.

Yet the classical economists went further, and showed that even if one country is more productive in *all* areas, then its people will *still* benefit from trading with people from a country that is less productive, across the board. In this scenario, each country specializes in its *comparative advantage*, which means the goods and services where it has the *relative* (not necessarily the absolute) strength.

At the individual level, this principle shows up when a pediatrician, for example, hires nurses to take patients' blood pressure, weight, and height, and to ask about symptoms, before the pediatrician enters the room. The doctor is actually better able to perform these routine tasks than the nurses, but it is more efficient for him to outsource these activities, freeing him up to see more patients per day than if he did everything himself. For another example, a lawyer might be a very fast typist, but it still makes sense for her to hire a secretary to handle her correspondence, send bills to clients, and so forth. Even though the lawyer would actually make a "better secretary" than the person she hired, she makes a *much* better attorney, and it is worthwhile

Let me just review these notes, Mr. Jones, and see if we can help you today ...

for her to concentrate on strict legal work, while her employee (the secretary) handles the tasks that don't require an intimate knowledge of the law. In this example, the attorney has the *absolute* advantage in both legal work and secretarial work, but she has a *comparative advantage* only in legal work. (Her employee has the absolute advantage in neither task, but the comparative advantage in secretarial work.)

The same principle of comparative advantage carries through to countries as a whole, as David Ricardo illustrated. For example, compared to India, Canada has the absolute advantage in both the production of aircraft parts *and* textiles, meaning that for every hour of labour time expended, a Canadian worker can produce more of either good compared to an Indian worker. This absolute advantage in both lines reflects the superior education and training, infrastructure, institutions, and amount of capital equipment with which the Canadian workers can augment their raw labour.

Even so, it nonetheless makes sense for Canadians to specialize in what they're *really* good at—such as producing components for jet aircraft—and import much of the clothes that they want to wear. Just as with our pediatrician and our lawyer, Canadian workers can enjoy a higher standard of living if they allow others (even those who aren't as productive) to perform some jobs, in order to free up the Canadian workers to focus on the niches in which their advantage is the greatest.

If all workers in each country were identical, no one would clamor for tariffs. By adopting free trade, a country makes its *average* citizen richer, and thus—if all citizens were identical—a move toward free trade would make *every* citizen richer. However, in the real world workers have different skills, and for this reason some pockets of workers can indeed be hurt by reducing existing tariffs. For example, if there were initially a high tariff barrier on foreign textiles, this would certainly "protect" Canadian workers in the textile industry. But their gains would be more than offset by the higher prices paid by Canadian consumers in general.

It is important to realize that protectionist barriers, such as tariffs and quotas, don't "protect" jobs in general, but merely protect jobs *in inefficient sectors*. If the Canadian government enacts a high enough tariff wall on foreign textiles, this would certainly "create jobs" in the Canadian textile industry. But it would simultaneously *destroy* jobs in Canadian export sectors. Consider: If the Canadian government makes it impossible for China and India to export their textiles to Canadian consumers, then these countries can't earn the currency with which to buy natural gas or automobiles produced in Canada. Ultimately, a country pays for its imports with its exports. If the Canadian government artificially expands certain sectors by protecting them from cheap foreign imports, it will simultaneously shrink other Canadian sectors that depend on exports. Tariff and quota barriers don't promote employment, they merely *rearrange* it. What's worse, they do so in an inefficient way, so that the average productivity of workers drops. Individual workers in the protected sectors may benefit, but Canadians in general become poorer. Writing in 2013, Mark Milke lamented the existence of tariffs on foods produced in the dairy and poultry sectors.

> There, tariffs on foreign imports range from 202% (skim milk) to 298% (butter); cheese, yogurt, ice cream and regular milk fall within that range. If Ottawa dropped the tariffs and ended the government-protected dairy and poultry cartels where supply is restricted and new competitors banned, consumers would see real drops in prices.[30]

As the above statistics illustrate, these protectionist measures make millions of Canadian consumers poorer (through higher dairy and poultry prices) while concentrating benefits (in the form of higher income) in the hands of a much smaller group of farmers.

Although embracing free trade with the entire world may seem too aggressive for some Canadians, the case for free trade with the United States should be obvious. Other nations around the world are forming their own free-trade blocs, with impressive results. Commenting on the growing integration of Europe into a free-trade region with no internal barriers on goods or workers, Leonard Waverman observed, "The U.S. and Canada, with little animosity and many similarities, have been discussing free trade for over 135 years!"[31] Waverman further reported that according to one estimate, a

---

30 Mark Milke (2013, February 9). Abolish the $3.6 Billion Tariff tax on the Poor. *Calgary Herald*. <http://www.fraserinstitute.org/research-news/news/commentaries/Abolish-the-$3-6-billion-tariff-tax-on-the-poor/>, as of April 15, 2014.

31 Leonard Waverman (1991). A Canadian Vision of North American Economic Integration. In Steven Globerman, ed., *Continental Accord: North American Economic Integration* (Fraser Institute): 36.

true bilateral free trade agreement (existing "free trade" agreements have many exceptions) between the United States and Canada would almost *double* Canadian trade with its southern neighbour, and would lead to a 9% gain in Canadian welfare.[32]

Not only international trade, but inter*provincial* trade, should be free from arbitrary government barriers. Most economists agree that one of the primary sources of U.S. economic strength is its federal constitutional prohibition on trade barriers among the individual states. In a Fraser Institute collection devoted to the problem of provincial barriers—covering such diverse goods as beer, agricultural products, labour, and commercial transportation—editor Filip Palda wrote:

> Interprovincial trade barriers are perhaps the biggest solvable economic problem that our politicians cannot bring themselves to solve. These barriers cost Canadians at least $6.5 billion a year in lost income... We do not know precisely how much larger the internal market would be if goods and services could flow freely. What we do know is that internal barriers raise the cost of doing business, increase taxes, destroy jobs, and make us less competitive. By lessening each province's dependence on other provinces, barriers also work against Canadian unity.[33]

Since Palda was writing back in 1994, the harm from Canada's provincial tariff barriers—levied against other Canadians—is much higher today.

The economic case for free trade has been firmly established for centuries: Overall productivity and living standards rise when nations specialize in those niches in which they have the comparative (that is, relative) advantage. Barriers to trade might benefit a privileged few in the "protected" industries, but only by making the consumers poorer.

Perhaps the most succinct argument for free trade was offered by the 19th century American economist Henry George, when he pointed out that in wartime, a naval power will impose a blockade on its enemy, trying to seal it off from imports. Yet in peacetime, a nation seeks to do the very same thing

---

32 Waverman: 43.

33 Filip Palda (1994). *Provincial Trade Wars: Why the Blockade Must End.* Fraser Institute: xi.

to itself, through tariff barriers. If everyone can see that blockading a nation is an aggressive and harmful act, then why do people still support such measures directed at their own population?

As with our other institutions, free trade also has numerous studies touting its benefits. For example, Daniel Griswold (2004) uses two different indices: The first is produced by Freedom House, a human rights group, which incorporates measures of civil liberties and political rights. The other is the Fraser Institute's Economic Freedom of the World Index's category on open-ness to trade and ability to conduct transactions with foreigners. Griswold reports that "the most economically open countries are three times more likely to enjoy full political and civil freedoms as those that are economically closed," while those "that are closed are nine times more likely to completely suppress civil and political freedoms as those that are open."[34]

---

34 Daniel Griswold (2004). *Trading Tyranny for Freedom: How Open Markets Till the Soil for Democracy.* Trade Policy Analysis No. 26 (January 6). <http://www.cato.org/publications/trade-policy-analysis/trading-tyranny-freedom-how-open-markets-till-soil-democracy>, as of April 15, 2014.

CHAPTER THREE

Economic myths and how they prevent progress

Knowledge is power

Armed with our ten principles of sound economic thinking from Chapter One, and the seven institutional prerequisites for prosperity from Chapter Two, in this final chapter we explode fifteen economic myths, supplementing our earlier discussion with hard facts. The myths below are grouped into two categories: Myths #1 through #9 are largely empirical, whereas Myths #10 through #15 are conceptual in nature. However, all of the myths need a good dose of reality to set the record straight.

Our purpose in this third chapter is not simply to provide banter for cocktail parties. Erroneous but widespread beliefs about the (alleged) efficacy of government action and the (alleged) shortcomings of voluntary activities lead the public to support harmful policies that retard economic progress. It is therefore crucial that Canadian citizens and policymakers alike understand our refutation of some of the most consequential of these myths.

Category 1: Myths based on empirical mistakes

Economic Myth #1

Reforming Canadian health care means a US system

Many Canadians are reluctant to entertain proposals for reforming the provision of health care services—especially if they seem to involve "market-based" and cost-saving mechanisms—because they fear this will jeopardize their cherished guarantee of universal access and coverage. In short, many Canadians are afraid that fiscally sensible reforms will lead to a U.S. system.

However, this fear is groundless. There is much room for improvement in the delivery of Canadian health care—in terms of saving money *and* boosting quality for recipients—while still retaining universal coverage. The simplest way to demonstrate this fact is to compare Canada with other countries that *also* have universal coverage. After adjusting health care spending for the ages of their populations, Canada (in 2011, the most recent year data are available) was at the top of the pack, as **Figure 3.1** illustrates.

Figure 3.1: Age-adjusted health spending (% GDP) in OECD countries with universal access, 2011

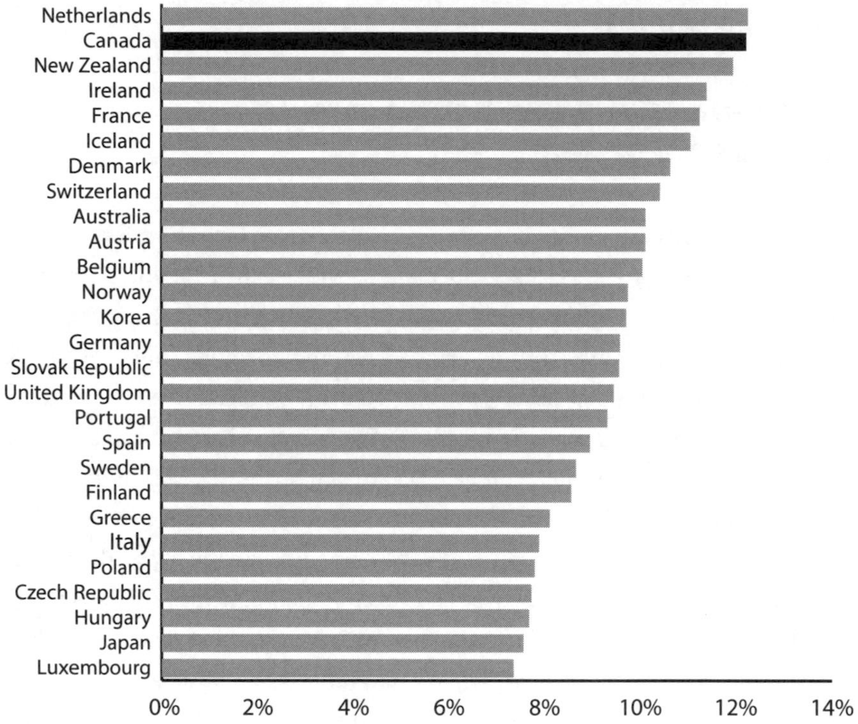

Source: OECD, 2013a; calculations by author.

As Figure 3.1 makes clear, it is difficult to claim that Canadian health care is underfunded. After adjusting for the different age distributions in their populations, Canada (in 2011) was just shy of tying the Netherlands for leading the world in the size of its economy devoted to health care spending. Right away, this fact proves that the shortcomings in Canadian health care are *not* due to an unwillingness to spend enough money; more money is not the answer, because Canada is already among the world's leaders in this respect.

Now we move to the obvious question: What is the *performance* of Canada's health care system, in light of the fact that it spends more than almost any other country in the relevant peer group?

The depressing answer is that Canada is woefully deficient on several objective measures. For example, **Figure 3.2** shows the number of doctors per 1,000 population (adjusting for age).

Figure 3.2: Practising doctors per 1,000 population, age-adjusted, 2011 or nearest year

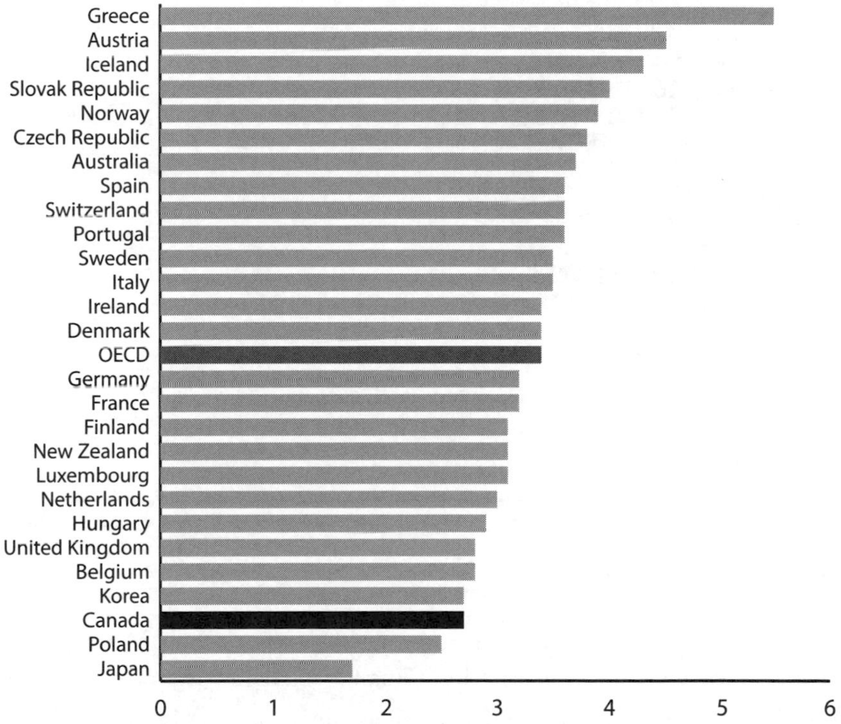

Source: OECD, 2013a; calculations by author.

As Figure 3.2 shows, Canada is near the bottom of the pack, with a lower availability of doctors than in most European nations. We see a similar pattern when it comes to the ubiquity of MRI machines per million of the population, as shown in **Figure 3.3**.

Figure 3.3: MRI units per million population (age-adjusted), 2011 or nearest year

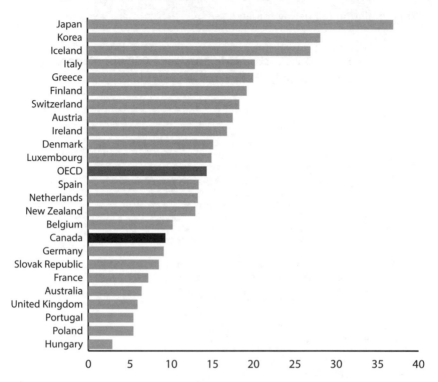

Source: OECD, 2013a; calculations by author.

Once again, on this criterion Canada falls below the mark of many OECD countries. Finally, in addition to looking at indirect indicators (such as number of doctors), we can compile data on *direct* health outcomes (such as survival rates for particular types of cancer) to see how Canada compares with other countries that provide universal access to their citizens. **Table 3.1** summarizes the results. As Table 3.1 shows, Canada's overall rank (the far right column) is only seventh, despite the fact that it spends more than almost any other country (adjusting for age) in this peer group. Recall from Figure 3.1 that Italy spends far less than Canada (7.9% of GDP versus 12.2%) and yet, at least according to the methodology in Table 3.1, Italy ranks five slots ahead of Canada in actual health outcomes.

Table 3.1: Performance of health systems in OECD countries with universal health access, 2011 (or latest year available)

	Mortality Amenable to Health Care, Rank 2007	Cancer survival			Short term in-hospital mortality		Avoidable admissions			Overall rank
		Five year relative survival rate or breast cancer, rank	Five year relative survival rate for cervical cancer, rank	Five year relative survival rate for colorectal cancer, rank	In-hospital case-fatality rates within 30 days, AMI, rank	In-hospital case-fatality rates within 30 days, ischemic stroke, rank	Uncontrolled diabetes hospital admission rate, rank	COPD hospital admission rate, rank	Asthma hospital admission rate, rank	
Sweden	5	5	5	8	2	7	9	10	5	1
Italy	3	*13*	*11*	*12*	9	8	1	3	1	2
Norway	9	6	2	9	2	4	5	14	7	3
Iceland	2	3	4	*12*	7	11	2	20	17	4
Netherlands	5	7	7	9	12	12	*14*	8	9	5
France	1	*13*	*11*	*12*	11	14	*14*	5	12	6
Canada	**11**	**1**	**9**	**6**	**7**	**19**	**6**	**12**	**2**	**7**
Japan	4	*13*	*11*	*12*	25	1	*14*	1	10	8
Australia	5	2	6	2	5	21	10	22	21	9
Finland	13	7	12	5	15	5	12	6	20	10
Switzerland	21	*13*	*11*	*12*	10	10	3	4	8	11
Austria	8	12	3	11	18	6	20	23	18	12
Denmark	20	15	8	15	1	3	13	21	11	13
Germany	15	10	15	4	23	9	17	16	4	14
New Zealand	17	4	14	7	2	14	15	24	24	15
Spain	9	*13*	*11*	*12*	21	22	7	15	16	16
Korea	18	9	1	1	23	2	21	18	25	17
Luxembourg	12	*13*	*11*	*12*	22	25	*14*	8	6	18
Belgium	21	11	9	3	16	16	16	17	15	19
Portugal	21	14	16	14	20	24	8	2	3	20
Ireland	16	18	18	13	12	20	11	25	13	21
Czech Republic	22	16	13	17	12	17	18	7	14	22
Poland	23	19	19	18	6	13	19	13	22	23
United Kingdom	18	16	17	16	19	23	4	19	19	24
Slovak Republic	24	*13*	*11*	*12*	16	26	*14*	11	26	25
Hungary	25	*13*	*11*	*12*	26	18	22	26	23	26

Notes: Overall rank compares the sum of average ranks for each category.

Not all information was available for all nations. Where data was unavailable, the rank of average values (universal countries) has been inserted in italics. All data are for 2011 or nearest year, 2006-2011 for cancer survival rates, unless otherwise noted.

Sources: OECD, 2013a; Gay et al., 2011; calculations by authors.

Beyond the fact that its overall outcome ranking lags well behind its spending, Canada does very poorly in its short term in-hospital mortality rate due to ischemic strokes (ranking 19th in the peer group of 26 total countries). To repeat, it would be one thing if Canadians endured a relatively unimpressive health care system in exchange for relatively low expenditures, but in fact they underperform several countries (all with universal coverage) even though they spend more than all countries except the Netherlands in this group.

If more spending is not the solution, how can Canadians reform their health care delivery system without sacrificing the commitment to universal access? Esmail and Walker (2008) provide some answers, looking at the other OECD countries for guidance. They conclude, "The models that produce superior results and cost less than Canada's monopoly-insurer, monopoly-provider system have: user fees; alternative, comprehensive, privately funded care; and private hospitals that compete for patient demand."[35]

Canadians can and should have a healthy debate about specific proposals to improve the delivery of health care. However, they must abandon the myth that the introduction of market-based reforms will necessarily spell the end of universal access. Most of the other OECD nations grant universal health coverage to their citizens as well, and yet they manage to deliver comparable (and in many respects superior) outcomes at lower cost.

---

35 Nadeem Esmail and Michael Walker (2008). *How Good Is Canadian Health Care? 2008 Report: An International Comparison of Health Care Systems.* Fraser Institute: 10.

Economic Myth #2

Canada spends considerably more on public education than the United States[36]

This myth is one that applies (though with different significance) to both Canadians *and* Americans. On the one hand, most Canadians probably believe—with pride—that in this country, education receives more generous funding from the government than in the ruggedly individualistic United States. Most Americans, for their part, probably believe that the "socialist" Canadian system "wastes" more tax dollars on poorly functioning schools than in the more efficiently run U.S. system. As it turns out, *both* views are false! In terms of both government oversight and funding levels, the Canadian educational system is much more decentralized than in the United States.

One of the starkest illustrations of the different models at work between the two countries, is the fact that Canada has no federal role, no federal ministry or department, and no federal cabinet position for K-12 education at all. Many Americans would be shocked to hear this, as they take it for granted that all modern "welfare state" countries (including Canada, of course) have extensive federal or central government involvement in K-12 education. Yet in Canada, this vital aspect of society is under the exclusive control and authority of the provinces. Furthermore, in many provinces the delivery responsibilities are decentralized to local and regional boards of education.

In contrast, the federal government in the United States is directly involved in K-12 education through both regulatory measures and direct spending. The United States has an entire federal department with over 4,200 employees and a Secretary of Education as part of the cabinet.[37]

Government at all levels in the United States spends more, too. In 2010, the U.S. spent 3.7% of GDP on public education versus 3.4% of GDP in Canada. *Total* spending (public and private) on K-12 was also higher in the

---

36 The discussion in Myth #2 closely follows that developed in Jason Clemens and Niels Veldhuis (2013). Hayekian Perspectives on Canada's Economic and Social Reforms of the 1990s. In Sandra J. Peart and David M. Levy (eds.), *F. A. Hayek and the Modern Economy: Economic Organization and Activity* (Palgrave Macmillan): 181–210.

37 Information from the White House as of July 2012, available at <www.whitehouse.gov/our-government/executive-branch>.

United States: 4.0% of GDP versus 3.9% in Canada. As these figures reveal, ironically *private* K-12 spending was slightly higher in Canada (0.5% of GDP) compared to the United States (0.3%).[38]

Once we adjust for student-body size, the difference in spending levels is even more striking. Adjusting for differences in currencies, in 2010 the United States (public and private) spent $11,826 per student on K-12 education. In contrast, the comparable figure for Canada was only $9,774[39] (**Figure 3.4**). Thus, the United States spent about one-fifth (21%) more per student in 2010 for primary and secondary education, and as we have seen, that difference arises from the higher level of *government* spending. Thus, the conventional wisdom is totally wrong: American taxpayers spend far more on public education than Canadians.

We should also point out that although the U.S. spends more on K-12 education than Canada, on most international tests, Canada performs at least as well as, and often much better than, the United States. For example, the OECD administers the Programme for International Student Assessment (PISA), which in 2006 gave U.S. students a science score of 489, compared to Canada's 534 and the OECD average of 500.[40]

Here, as in health care, it turns out that "throwing more money" at the issue doesn't necessarily mean better results. As we've seen, Canadians devote a smaller share of their economy to education than Americans do, and yet Canadian students typically outperform Americans. Before calling for spending increases in Canada, those concerned about improving education should first understand the traits that currently set it apart from the U.S. approach, since "more money" is obviously not one of them.

---

38 Data from OECD (2013b). *Education at a Glance 2013: OECD Indicators.* OECD Publishing. <http://www.oecd.org/edu/eag2013%20(eng)--FINAL%2020%20June%202013.pdf>, as of April 15, 2014. The specific measure is "primary, secondary, and post-secondary non-tertiary" education spending.
39 All figures are quoted in equivalent 2008 U.S. dollars converted using Purchasing Power Parity (PPP) for GDP based on full-time equivalents. The specific measure is "primary, secondary, and post-secondary non-tertiary" education spending per student, including private and public spending. Data from OECD (2013b).
40 See Table A5.1 at <http://www.oecd.org/document/9/0,3343,en_2649_39263238_41266761_1_1_1_1,00.html>.

Figure 3.4: Public, private, and total spending on K-12 education, Canada versus United States, 2010

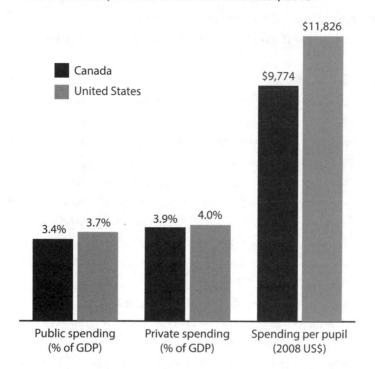

Source: OECD, 2013b.

Economic Myth #3

Government workers are poorly paid compared to their private sector counterparts

It is common for Canadians to bemoan the plight of the government worker, who is allegedly scraping by on a pittance, while his or her private-sector counterpart enjoys a plush lifestyle financed by powerful corporations. In reality, Canadian government workers tend to be paid more, *and* they generally have more advantageous non-wage perks.

One of the difficulties in comparing wages among workers in government versus the private sector is that there are many factors that go into the determination of a wage; it's difficult to truly make the comparison apples to apples. Even so, there are studies that use regression analysis to attempt to isolate the difference in pay between the government and private sector. For example, Palacios and Clemens (2013) report: "After controlling for such factors as gender, age, marital status, education, tenure, size of firm, province, city, type of job, and industry," government workers at all levels "enjoyed a 12.0% wage premium, on average, over their private sector counterparts."

Thus, we see that the common perception of underpaid government workers is simply not borne out by the data, at least after we control for obvious drivers of wage differences (such as age and education). What's more, Palacios and Clemens find that *non-wage* benefits also appear to be more desirable for the government workers versus their private sector counterparts. For example, 88.2% of government workers were covered by a registered pension plan, while only 24.0% of private sector workers were covered (**Figure 3.5**). Furthermore, 94.0% of the government sector registered pensions were "defined benefit" plans (meaning that the retiree is guaranteed a certain level of retirement income), rather than "defined contribution" plans (meaning that the worker is merely guaranteed that the employer will contribute a certain dollar amount to the plan, but the amount this yields in retirement is uncertain). In contrast, only 52.3% of private sector registered pensions were defined benefit plans. Because they involve less risk to the retiree, defined benefit plans are generally considered preferable (other things equal), meaning that the government sector pensions plans were more generous in this respect.

Figure 3.5: Percentage of employees covered by a registered pension plan in 2011

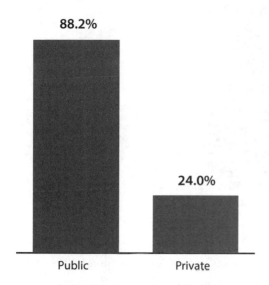

Source: Palacios and Clemens, 2013.

Yet there are still more advantages: On average, government workers retire about 2.5 years earlier than private sector counterparts, and were much less likely to lose their jobs in 2011 (**Figures 3.6** and **3.7**).

Figure 3.6: Average retirement age in Canada, 2007–2011

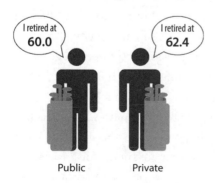

Source: Palacios and Clemens, 2013.

Figure 3.7: Job loss as a percentage of employment in 2011

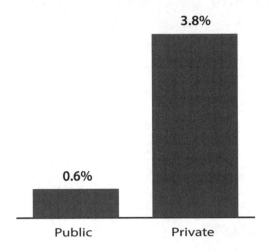

Source: Palacios and Clemens, 2013

Although there are other aspects of a job's total compensation package that might mitigate some of these disparities, the above data suggest that government workers enjoy high compensation compared to their private sector counterparts.

This result should not surprise us. After all, government workers are paid through taxation, meaning the connection between the payment and "customer" is much more tenuous than in the private sector. This means that there are few (if any) competitive pressures on government operations, since they don't need to convince their "customers" to continue patronizing them, as a private business does. Furthermore, managers in the government sector do not directly benefit from developing a "lean" labour force. Their different institutional settings allow government workers to enjoy relative "overpayment" for work comparable to that of their private sector peers, because in the private sector an individual firm would suffer losses if it didn't carefully match pay with performance.

These observations do not imply that, say, public school teachers are poor workers. Rather, we are simply pointing to the different incentive structures to explain why the data show an advantage for government employees. The government does not need to worry about costs as much as private sector employers, because it derives its funding from involuntary taxation. Furthermore, no individual manager in the government sector has the incentive to produce the same amount of "output" (however measured) for a lower expenditure, because this typically would simply mean that his or her budget would be cut in the next fiscal period.

Canadians should therefore abandon the myth that government workers are relatively underpaid, and deserving of a raise (at taxpayer expense, of course). Both economic theory and empirical research suggest the opposite, which also means that where possible, goods and services should be provided through the private sector, where the institutional framework is designed to channel workers into their most productive niches.

Economic Myth #4

The rich don't pay their fair share in taxes

A particularly harmful economic myth is the notion that the wealthy are undertaxed. As we will see, not only do typical upper-income households pay more in taxes than other households, but they even pay more taxes as a share of their income. The myth that the rich don't pay their "fair share" is harmful to all Canadians—rich, middle class, and poor alike—because it leads the public to support very inefficient tax policies that hinder economic growth and job creation.

One obvious starting point to assess the fairness of the tax code is to look at the marginal rates and thresholds for the federal income tax. This information (pertaining to 2013) is presented in **Table 3.2**.

We see that the federal income tax code is very "progressive," meaning that it taxes income earned in higher brackets at a higher marginal rate. For example, someone with an income of $200,000 would pay 29 cents of every additional dollar earned to the federal government in income tax, while someone with an income of $40,000 would only pay 15 cents of his additional dollar earned in federal income tax. Furthermore, those earning less than $11,038 were completely exempt from federal income tax.

However, federal personal income taxes are not the whole story, because lower income groups still pay substantial amounts to governments at all levels in the form of local taxes, provincial sales taxes, federal payroll taxes, and others. We can get a much more comprehensive assessment of the

Table 3.2: Federal personal income tax rates and thresholds, 2013

	Threshold or rate
Basic personal income tax exemption	$11,038
Lowest personal income tax rate	15%
Threshold for 2nd rate	$43,561
2nd rate	22%
Threshold for 3rd rate	$87,123
3rd rate	26%
Threshold for 4th rate	$135,054
4th rate	29%

Source: KPMG, 2014.

true burden of Canadian taxation by inspecting **Table 3.3**, which shows the percentage of total tax receipts collected at the federal, provincial, and local levels allocated across various tax types, as well as the distribution of taxation among the various thresholds of income earners. Some of this information is represented in graphical form in **Figure 3.8**.

Table 3.3 should disabuse any Canadian of the myth that the rich don't pay their fair share in taxes. For example, the top quintile (i.e. 20%) of earners pay a whopping 64.7% of all individual income taxes collected in Canada, even though they only earn 47.5% of the total cash income. The top 0.1% of earners—just one one-thousandth of the population—pay 5.4% of *all* Canadian taxes, while only earning 3.3% of total cash income.

As these data indicate, the rich—defined as those earning high incomes—bear a disproportionately large share of the total Canadian tax burden, even adjusting for their disproportionate share of income. These remarks do not minimize the significant hardships faced by lower- and middle-income households, who also pay significant amounts to governments at various levels, a burden that is especially difficult during sluggish economic times. Yet the proper policy response to deal with such concerns is *not* to make the tax code even more onerous on higher earners, as this will reduce the incentives for economic growth and job creation. Rather, the solution is to eliminate unnecessary government spending and counterproductive tax designs that impose economic burdens with no corresponding revenue. (We explain this latter concept in greater detail in our Myth #11.)

Table 3.3: Distribution of federal, provincial, and local taxes in Canada, by quintile and tax type (2013, preliminary estimate)

	Cash income	Individual income tax	Social Security, pension, medical & hospital tax	Corporate income tax	Other taxes	All taxes
Lowest Quintile	4.8	0.6	2.9	2.1	3.0	1.9
Second Quintile	9.9	3.8	9.4	9.0	9.7	6.8
Middle Quintile	15.2	10.5	18.3	14.3	17.6	13.8
Fourth Quintile	22.7	20.5	27.5	18.2	26.7	22.1
Top Quintile	47.5	64.7	42.0	56.4	62.7	55.4
All	100.0	100.0	100.0	100.0	100.0	100.0
Addendum						
80-89	15.6	16.4	11.3	18.7	15.4	16.0
90-94	9.9	11.7	7.6	10.5	9.9	10.4
95-99	14.1	19.9	15.6	11.5	15.3	16.4
Top 1 Percent	9.3	18.0	22.8	2.9	13.1	14.0
Top 0.1 Percent	3.3	7.0	0.5	9.5	5.0	5.4

Notes: Social security and pension tax includes both the employee and employer contributions.

Other taxes include sales taxes, property taxes, excise taxes, auto, fuel and motor vehicle licence taxes, import duties and natural resources levies.

Source: Fraser Institute, Canadian Tax Simulator, 2013.

Figure 3.8: Quintile shares of income and total taxes, 2013

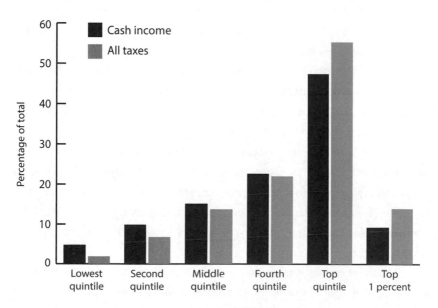

Source: Fraser Institute, Canadian Tax Simulator, 2013.

Economic Myth #5

The minimum wage helps underpaid, underskilled workers

Whenever there is a push to raise the minimum wage, proponents explain that it is impossible for someone, let alone a working parent, to support a household at the current level. The public picks up this image, thinking the typical minimum wage recipient is a middle-aged person with few job skills, trapped in an unrewarding position and unable to get ahead because of the meager pay. Most Canadians naturally conclude that it would surely be a fair thing to increase the take-home pay of these struggling workers, at the expense of a slight reduction in business earnings.

Natural though such a conclusion might be, it is utterly wrong, both conceptually and empirically. In the first place, raising the minimum wage increases *unemployment* among unskilled workers. Think about it: At the original wage level, employers wanted to hire a certain number of workers to fill low-skill positions, while a certain number of workers applied for those spots. By mandating a higher wage, the government will cause employers to want *fewer* workers, while more job-seekers will be interested in finding work. Consequently, there will be an even greater mismatch between the number of openings and the number of applicants, raising the unemployment rate among unskilled workers.

These worries aren't merely theoretical. As Godin and Veldhuis (2009) summarize, fourteen academic studies examined the impact of minimum wage increases in Canadian provinces. They concluded that a 10% increase in the minimum wage is likely to decrease employment by 3 to 6% for young workers aged 15 to 24. Furthermore, for workers with pay at or near the existing minimum wage, the impact is more acute, with employment losses of up to 20%. (Keep in mind that not all workers aged 15 to 24 earn the minimum wage, which explains the discrepancy.) This mechanism is at least partially responsible for the high unemployment rates among young workers, compared to the general labour force.

As these considerations indicate, the typical minimum wage earner is *not* the head of a poor household, struggling to make a living. Rather, 59% are between 15 and 24, and nearly 90% live at home with a family. Even many of the adults earning minimum wage are not the breadwinners of the household, but instead have taken part-time work to supplement the family's income.[41]

There is yet another problem with the popular understanding of the minimum wage issue. Rather than viewing these positions as "dead end jobs," and consequently insisting on a higher wage floor to provide a "decent living" to the workers, people should view minimum wage positions as *gateway jobs* to a better career. For example, Smith and Vavrichek (1992) document that more than 60% of minimum wage workers experience a raise, typically of about 20%, within a year after being first hired. According to Long (1999), more than 80% of initially minimum wage workers will end up earning more than the minimum wage within the first two years of employment.

You're welcome. We raised the minimum wage to help you out.

As these data reveal, the standard public discourse on the minimum wage is woefully misinformed. In a market economy, it is normal and healthy for young people with minimal education and work experience to take entry-level positions. Employers are willing to "take a gamble" on these unknown individuals because the starting pay is so modest. Over time, as these workers develop good habits and experience, they will receive promotions and pay increases.

Minimum wage legislation is a top-down government price control that interferes with the voluntary decisions of workers and employers. The natural market forces of

---

41 Data on minimum wage earners from Statistics Canada (2010). *Minimum Wage. Perspectives on Labour and Income.* Catalogue no. 75-001-XIE.

competition provide a tendency for workers to be paid what they are truly worth; this is why most workers receive far more than the minimum wage. Policymakers are not doing any favours for the poor when they raise the minimum wage; they are merely remove the bottom rung from the ladder of economic mobility. Minimum wage laws thus prevent less skilled workers from getting the entry-level jobs that provide them the experience and new skills they need to move up the economic ladder.

Economic Myth #6

Today's poor are tomorrow's poor

Many Canadians assume that "the poor" is a static group of the same individuals, such that people who are poor today will most likely be poor in the future (at least absent government assistance). This myth often accompanies a corollary view, that "the rich" are the same people through time.

In fact, Canada exhibits vibrant income mobility, so that the poor are not condemned by private enterprise to a lifetime of poverty, but instead enjoy opportunities to improve their situation. On the other hand, today's rich often find themselves relegated to a lower status in the future, as a dynamic marketplace changes and their activities are no longer as handsomely rewarded.

Beyond the general desirability of learning the proper facts, it is particularly important to shatter the myth of fixed income classes because it underlies the public's support for government redistribution programs. As we have hopefully explained in the rest of this book, the taxation necessary to *finance* such programs provides a drag on economic growth and job creation, thereby undermining the very mechanism that will provide today's poor with a legitimate escape route. That's why it's so important for the public to understand just how dynamic Canada's income classes are.

The fundamental problem with the typical media treatment and public perception of income classifications is that they conflate a *snapshot in time* with a *condition through time*. For example, it is quite common for commentators to remark that between two dates—such as 1990 and 2000—"the top 20%" saw a larger income increase than "the bottom 20%." Such descriptions are very misleading, because these are not the same group of people in both years.

To drive home the point, imagine the following thought experiment: Suppose initially there are five people in the economy, named Albert, Bob, Christine, Douglas, and Elizabeth. In 1990 they earn $10,000, $20,000, $20,000, $20,000, and $100,000, respectively. Thus we would say that in 1990, "the bottom 20%"—in other words, Albert—earned only one-tenth as much as "the top 20%"—in other words, Elizabeth.

Fast forward to the year 2000. Now, Albert earns $200,000; Bob, Christine, and Douglas each earn $25,000; but Elizabeth for some reason sees her income drop to a mere $11,000. Clearly, in this hypothetical example, there is great income mobility for the poor, while the rich cannot rest on their laurels. Yet the way such figures are typically reported in the media, Canadians would learn, "From 1990 to 2000, the bottom quintile saw its income rise 10%. The middle three quintiles saw their incomes rise 25%. And the richest fifth of the country saw their incomes rise a whopping 100%, enjoying far more gains than anyone else." Clearly such reporting—though technically accurate—would paint the *opposite* picture of what had really occurred.

Although our hypothetical story above is exaggerated for illustrative purposes, it does serve to warn us about the conventional reporting on income classes. In fact, longitudinal studies of given groups (as opposed to static snapshots taken at different intervals) show just how upwardly mobile the Canadian economy can be. In a 2012 Fraser Institute study, Lammam, Karabegović, and Veldhuis looked at Canadians over different time periods and reached some startling conclusions.[42]

For example, from 1990 to 2000, 83% of Canadians who started in the bottom quintile moved to a higher quintile. From 1990 to 2009, 21% of those who started in the bottom 20% had reached the top 20% of income earners. (See **Figure 3.9** for the full details on the fate of the bottom 20 percent after 19 years.) On the other hand, of those in the top 20% in 1990, 36% moved down at least one income group by 2009.

Beyond the *relative* movement in the income distribution compared to the rest of the population, the *absolute* movement in income is also impressive—and paints a much better picture of the plight of the (initially) poor in Canada. The average income of those initially in the bottom fifth in 1990 had grown an impressive 635% by 2009, while the average income of those initially

---

42 In the statistics referring to Canadian mobility, "income" is defined as wages and salaries.

Figure 3.9: Where the bottom 20% in 1990 were 19 years later in 2009

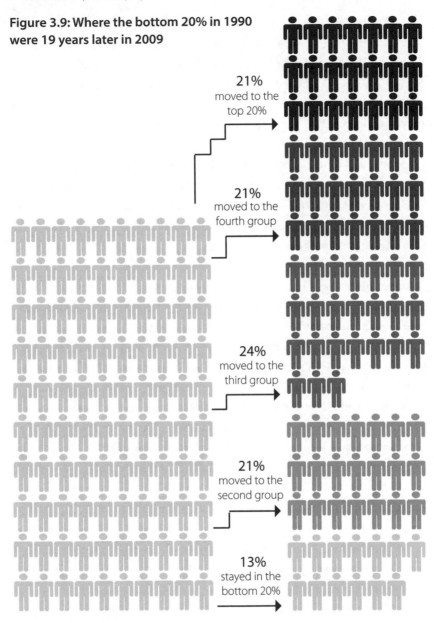

21% moved to the top 20%

21% moved to the fourth group

24% moved to the third group

21% moved to the second group

13% stayed in the bottom 20%

Note: Income is measured by wages and salaries

Source: Lammam, Karabegovic, and Veldhuis, 2012.

in the top fifth grew by only 23% over the same 19 years. In 1990, the average income of individuals in the highest fifth was 13 times that of individuals initially in the lowest group. Yet by 2009, those who had been in the highest group back in 1990 now had an average income only twice that of those who had been in the lowest group in 1990.

As these data indicate, being relatively poor—in other words, earning a lower income than most others—in Canada is *not* a prison sentence. Over time, most of those who initially start in the lowest income group eventually rise out of it, and indeed tend to experience a greater percentage increase in their wages and salaries than those who initially started out higher in the distribution.

It is important to dispel the myth that "today's poor are tomorrow's poor." Everyone enjoys hearing anecdotes of, say, an immigrant cab driver who pinches pennies in order to send his son to medical school. As the statistics presented in this section show, such stories aren't fairy tales; people really *do* enjoy economic mobility in Canada. Government policies can either aid or hinder such mobility. The danger is that allegedly egalitarian government programs—which redistribute income from the high earners to those making very little—will sabotage the very engine of capitalism that produces lasting improvements for everyone, especially the poor.

Economic Myth #7

Economic growth and environmental protection are incompatible

There is a widely held but false view that a strong economy and a clean environment are in conflict with each other. Many critics of private enterprise challenge its very premise as undermining the environment, and recommend a fundamental shift in societal values—away from "consumerism" and a narrow focus on jobs and output. Often these critics of the market will recommend strong government measures to force these changes upon the rest of the population, when their efforts at voluntary persuasion are not enough.

Environmental critics of capitalism are prevalent in every industrialized country. In Canada, traditionally the perspective has come from those advocating a "conserver society," implying that left to its own devices, a market economy would squander our natural heritage and leave a spoiled environment to our descendants. One of the leading institutional voices for the conserver perspective was the Science Council of Canada (which existed from 1966 to 1993). Another major source spreading the "conserver society" position for a Canadian audience was the four-volume report produced by the "Gamma group," academics who were affiliated with McGill University and the University of Montreal.[43]

For an example of the perspective of these groups, consider the following quotation from the Science Council in 1977: "A Conserver Society…is a society which…questions the ever-growing per capita demand for consumer goods, artificially encouraged by modern marketing techniques."[44]

Or consider the broader critique of capitalism offered by the Gamma group in this typical condemnation:

> The unlimited marketing of goods leads to a cumulative reduction in the pleasure of people because of the conspicuous external diseconomies produced, noise, pollution, urban congestion, etc…Many would argue that the market, rather than being a "want-satisfying mechanism" has become a "want-creating mechanism" principally through marketing and advertising.[45]

Yet another icon of this perspective, familiar to most Canadians, is Dr. David Suzuki, a professor of genetics at the University of British Columbia from 1963 to 2001, who has spent decades championing citizen and government action to protect the environment from the normal operations of capitalism. Suzuki tells his followers "you have the power" to conserve energy (through use of compact fluorescent light bulbs, for example), and in 2008 told a crowd of McGill University students, in the context of the threat of climate change: "What I would challenge you to do is to put a lot of effort into trying to see whether there's a legal way of throwing our so-called leaders into jail because what they're doing is a criminal act."[46]

---

43 See John F. Chant et al. (1990). The Economics of the Conserver Society. In Walter Block (ed.), *Economics and the Environment: A Reconciliation* (Fraser Institute): 2–3.

44 Science Council of Canada (1977). *Canada as Conserver Society: Resource Uncertainties and the Need for New Technologies*. Science Council of Canada: 14.

45 As quoted by Chant et al. (1990): 7–8.

46 Craig Offman (2008, February 7). Jail Politicians Who Ignore Climate Science: Suzuki. *The National Post*. <http://www.nationalpost.com/news/story.html?id=290513>, as of April 15, 2014.

Contrary to these (typical) claims, both theory and history show that strong economic growth, embedded in a capitalist framework, is the recipe for a *healthy* environment. For example, **Table 3.4** shows the 2012 country rankings from the World Economic Forum's *Environmental Performance Index* (EPI). This is an index compiled by the Yale Center for Environmental Law and Policy. It looks at indicators such as child mortality, particulate matter concentrations, carbon dioxide per capita, pressure on coastal shelf fishing pressure, and many others to determine a country's EPI score on the two broad categories of environmental health and ecosystem vitality.[47]

Table 3.4: World Economic Forum's Environmental Peformance Index rankings, 2012

Rank	EPI classification	Country
1		Switzerland
2		Latvia
3		Norway
4		Luxembourg
5	Strongest Performers	Costa Rica
6		France
7		Austria
8		Italy
9		United Kingdom
9		Sweden
37	Strong Performers	Canada
49	Modest Performers	United States
121		Tajikistan
122		Eritrea
123		Libyan Arab Jamahiriya
124		Bosnia and Herzegovina
125		India
126		Kuwait
127	Weakest Performers	Yemen
128		South Africa
129		Kazakhstan
130		Uzbekistan
131		Turkimenistan
132		Iraq

Source: Emerson et al., 2012.

47 The methodology behind the Environmental Performance Index is available at <http://epi.yale.edu/epi2012/methodology>.

Table 3.4 summarizes the top and bottom performers in the 2012 ranking. As it shows, the top performers were, generally speaking, countries with advanced economies and high per capita incomes. In contrast, the worst performers were (generally speaking) economically underdeveloped countries, or those wracked by military conflict. Nothing in Table 3.4 would suggest that government policies promoting market-based economic growth were in any way incompatible with environmental protection. If anything, the Yale rankings paint the opposite picture, namely that countries with authoritarian governments are associated with poor environmental scores.

As we have explained in the Introduction to this book, scores of studies show the tight connection between objective measures of economic freedom and economic growth. There are studies that also document a correlation between economic freedom and environmental quality. For example, Michael Stroup considered the wealthy OECD countries and gauged their environmental quality in terms of (standard) measures of air and water pollution, as well as greenhouse gas emissions. He then compared these results to the countries' scores on indices of economic and political freedom. After controlling for factors such as per-capita income, population, and urbanization, Stroup found that those countries with higher index scores on economic and political freedom *also* tended to have a higher environmental score.[48]

In a similar study, Brett D. Schaefer compared countries' scores on the Heritage Foundation/Wall Street Journal's *Index of Economic Freedom* as well as their performance on the Environmental Sustainability Index, a composite of 21 indicators of environmental stewardship that was co-developed by the Yale Center for Environmental Law and Policy. As with Stroup's analysis, Schaefer too found a strong correlation between the two measures, suggesting that economic freedom (and hence economic growth) is consistent with environmental protection.[49]

It should not be surprising that wealthy, capitalist countries tend to score well on objective measures of environmental quality, while relatively

---

48 Michael Stroup (2007). *The Influence of Capitalism and Democracy on Air Emissions among OECD Countries.* Working Paper (October 15). Available at <http://www.cob.sfasu.edu/mstroup/Pollution_10_15.pdf>

49 Brett D. Schaefer (2005). *Proposals for an Environmental Indicator for the MCA Should Be Resisted.* Heritage Backgrounder #1896 (November 14). <http://www.heritage.org/research/reports/2005/11/proposals-for-an-environmental-indicator-for-the-mca-should-be-resisted>, as of April 15, 2014.

undeveloped and authoritarian regimes tend to perform poorly. This is because environmental quality—such as smog-free air and clean drinking water—is a desirable but scarce good that a country can only afford if it is wealthy enough.

People often romanticize the past, thinking that the world must have been a "cleaner" place before the modern economy spoiled it. Yet consider science author Dixy Lee Ray's recollections of her childhood:

> The world in which I spent my early years was a very smelly place. The prevailing odors were of horse manure, human sweat, and unwashed bodies. A daily shower was unknown; at most there was the Saturday night bath. Indoors the air was generally musty and permeated by the sweetly acrid stench of kerosene lamps and coal fires. It was the era of the horse and buggy, the outhouse, and dirt. Depending upon the weather, it was either dusty or muddy ... Mr. Henry Ford made a greater contribution to public health than most practitioners of science by introducing an affordable auto—which led to the eventual elimination of horse manure from public streets.[50]

Thus we see that as a country grows richer through sustained economic growth, its citizens will not only enjoy better diets, medical care, transportation, and entertainment, but they will *also* "buy" a cleaner environment. This has certainly been the case in Canada, where objective measures of air quality in most regions have improved greatly since just the 1970s. In a 2012 study, Joel Wood compiled numerous statistics to demonstrate the impressive results, some of which are summarize in **Figure 3.10**.

As Figure 3.10 shows, over the last few decades, concentrations of nitrous dioxide (58%), carbon monoxide (86%), and sulfur dioxide (75%) have fallen drastically, while the concentration of ground-level ozone has fallen modestly (11%). During the same period, Canadian real GDP has grown significantly (94%). Clearly, economic growth in Canada has been consistent with cleaner air.

---

50 Dixy Lee Ray with Lou Guzzo (1990). *Trashing the Planet: How Science can Help Us Deal with Acid Rain, Depletion of the Ozone, and Nuclear Waste (Among Other Things)*. Regnery Gateway: 14.

Figure 3.10: Measures of air quality versus real GDP, Canada, 1981–2009

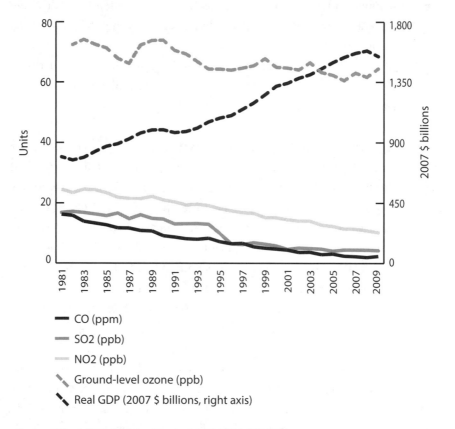

CO (ppm)
SO2 (ppb)
NO2 (ppb)
Ground-level ozone (ppb)
Real GDP (2007 $ billions, right axis)

Sources: Wood, 2012; Statistics Canada, CANSIM Table 380-0064.

There is a similar story when it comes to Canada's bodies of water. Joel Wood summarizes this in a report for the Fraser Institute:

> When we examine evidence from individual provinces over the long term, it is clear that, for many forms of pollution, water quality has improved greatly since the 1970s. In Ontario, total phosphorus has generally decreased in lakes and rivers since the 1970s. There has also been a general decline in mercury, PCBs, and many other toxic substances in the waters of Ontario and Quebec. Another example of improving water quality is the return to pre-settlement levels of total phosphorus in Lake Osoyoos in British Columbia. Bacteria levels

are decreasing in major Alberta rivers from improvements to sewage treatment. Due to improvements in the bleaching process used in British Columbia's pulp and paper mills, the province's rivers have seen a significant decrease in chloride levels since the 1980s. Evidence from Ontario suggests that pesticides and pharmaceuticals in drinking water and chloride in rivers from road salt are currently not at a level to prompt concern for water quality.[51]

Economic Myth #8

Natural resources are scarce and we will eventually run out, so the government should carefully ration their usage

Many critics of capitalism will concede that markets do a decent job of providing televisions, cars, and computers, but (they claim) government oversight is necessary when it comes to exhaustible resources. In Canada, with its rich heritage of natural resources, many people simply assume that private ownership and the profit motive lead to a rapid overdevelopment without adequate consideration of the needs of future generations.

In contrast to this typical view, many economists make the *opposite* case, arguing that private property rights actually give *more* incentives for the preservation of natural resources, compared to government management. For example, these economists blame the pollution of the air, forests, and bodies of water on the fact that these are (typically) considered communal resources legally owned by the government, meaning that they are in effect managed by temporary caretakers (government officials) who have no long-term ownership interest in the value of the property. Walter Block explains:

> Canadians who wonder what all the fuss is about when environmentalists raise alarms about the effects of acid rain on the forests react with outrage when the neighbour's dog performs *squatus smellibus* on their own front lawns... If the same dog-owning neighbour happens to own

---

51 Wood (2013). *Canadian Environmental Indicators—Water*. Fraser Institute: iii-iv.

an industrial plant that dumps a chemical effluent on some remote forest land, we have little reaction, even if we know about it. After all, the forest land isn't our private property. It's government land.[52]

For another example, consider the list of animals allegedly needing government protection from rapacious poachers and other human activities: historically this list included the bald eagle, the African white rhino, and the humpback whale. In contrast, no one ever worries about cattle or chickens going extinct, even though humans consume them in large quantities every year. What is it that makes one set of creatures vulnerable, while the others flourish? One key difference is that the former are (typically) unable to be owned and therefore bred in a commercial operation, whereas the latter are treated as private property. Private farmers and ranchers, as well as the owners of private fisheries, have the proper incentives to maintain a perpetual stock of the various animals, not out of an abstract concern for the needs of "future generations," but because of the bottom line: If farmers foolishly slaughtered chickens at a faster rate than they could naturally reproduce, the price of chickens would ultimately skyrocket as the supply dwindled. So long as there are adequate property rights in the various resources, we need never fear "overdevelopment" of cattle, trees, or trout.

One particularly poignant way to drive home this point is to chart the "total proved reserves" of finite resources, such as crude oil and natural gas, as we have done in **Figure 3.11**. As Figure 3.11 shows, global proved reserves of oil and gas have *increased* 130% and 161%, respectively, from 1980-2011. During this same period, cumulative oil *production* was some 842 billion barrels, while cumulative (dry) natural gas production was 2,595 trillion cubic feet. In other words, not only did the absolute stockpile of proved reserves of oil and gas increase over the three decades, but this occurred while the world *consumed* more than the entire 1980 total reserves of each.

How is this possible? How can the reserves of a finite resource *increase* over time, even as the world exploits it? The answer is that "proved reserves" are not an estimate of the physical amount of oil and gas on Earth, but instead refer to the *known* reserves that can be recovered under current conditions. Energy companies engage in long-term exploration and development projects

---

52 Block (1990). Environmental Problems, Private Property Rights Solutions. In Block: 281.

Figure 3.11: Worldwide proved reserves of crude oil and natural gas, 1980–2011

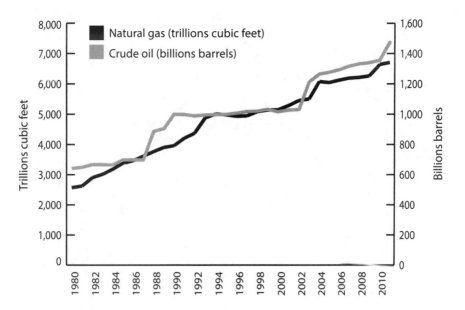

Source: US Energy Information Administration at
http://www.eia.gov/cfapps/ipdbproject/IEDIndex3.cfm.

to locate new reserves, but they are guided—just as other entrepreneurs are—by the price system. Up to a point, it makes sense to devote the time of geologists, chemists, and other workers to finding more oil and gas reserves, but after a sizable cushion has been established, these scarce inputs are devoted elsewhere.

One way of illustrating the "cushion" that humanity enjoys—and to evaluate the ability of markets to plan for the future—is to examine the "total years worth" of crude oil and natural gas, meaning we take worldwide proved reserves and divide by that year's usage of the resource in production. We have done this in **Figure 3.12.**

As Figure 3.12 shows, in 1980 the world had 27.5 years of reserves of crude oil at then-current rates of oil production, while it had 48.2 years of natural gas (using "dry natural gas" production rates). According to a naïve—yet

Figure 3.12: Worldwide "years' worth" of proved reserves of crude oil and natural gas, 1980–2011

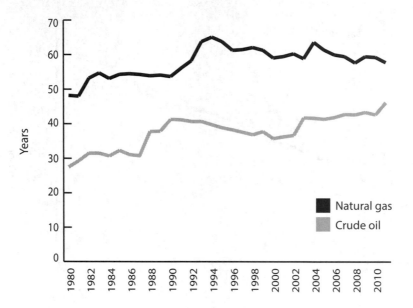

Source: US Energy Information Administration at
http://www.eia.gov/cfapps/ipdbproject/IEDIndex3.cfm.

very popular—way of interpreting such facts, governments around the world should have engaged in massive funding of "alternative" energy sources, since humans were on course to literally run out of oil in the year 2008.

Yet as the figure shows, no such catastrophe occurred. Despite the continual consumption of the finite stockpiles of oil and gas, the "years worth" of both commodities generally *increased* over the decades, ending at 46.2 and 57.8 years, respectively. To repeat, this is a natural and straightforward feature of capitalism: If experts in the industry foresaw a looming energy crisis, this would push up prices *now* (thus rationing current consumption) and would give the incentive to locate additional deposits.[53]

Private enterprise contains incentives for experts to locate more supplies of natural resources as they become needed. Governments do not need to take any special measures to conserve them.

---

53 The rising prices would also spur the development of substitutes, without the explicit guidance of government "alternative energy" programs.

Economic Myth #9

Canadians are more generous than Americans

Although many Canadians like to pride themselves on being more socially conscious than their selfish neighbours to the south, the truth is that Americans tend to give more to charity than Canadians. In a 2013 study for the Fraser Institute based on data from the 2011 tax year, McIntyre and Lammam document that whether a higher percentage of tax filers donate to charity in the United States (26.0%) versus Canada (22.9%), while the total amount of charitable giving as a fraction of aggregate income is more than twice as high in the United States (1.33%) versus Canada (0.64%). In absolute dollar terms, the average contribution to charity in the United States was US$4,596, while in Canada it was much lower at CDN$1,519. **Table 3.5** shows the breakdown of Canadian charitable giving at the provincial level.

Table 3.5: Generosity Index, Canadian results and rankings, 2011 tax year

	% taxfilers donating to charity		% aggregate income donated to charity		Average charitable donations	
	%	Rank	%	Rank	Amount ($)	Rank
British Columbia	21.7	7	0.75	3	1,889	2
Alberta	23.9	5	0.78	2	2,321	1
Saskatchewan	24.9	2	0.72	5	1,636	5
Manitoba	25.9	1	0.89	1	1,698	4
Ontario	24.1	4	0.73	4	1,714	3
Quebec	21.2	8	0.30	11	655	13
New Brunswick	20.7	10	0.57	7	1,233	8
Nova Scotia	22.2	6	0.53	8	1,169	9
Prince Edward Island	24.9	2	0.63	6	1,141	11
Newfoundland & Labrador	20.9	9	0.44	9	1,021	12
Yukon	20.5	11	0.32	10	1,164	10
Northwest Territories	15.5	12	0.27	12	1,348	7
Nunavut	9.3	13	0.22	13	1,594	6

Source: McIntyre and Lammam, 2013: Table 1.

As the table indicates, the provincial ranking of charitable giving differs according to the criterion. For example, Manitoba leads the provinces in terms of the percentage of tax filers who give, and the percentage of income donated. However, Alberta ranks highest in terms of the dollar amount of the average charitable donation in tax year 2011. Yet to repeat, none of the provinces comes close to the United States in terms of percentage of income donated, or the average dollar amount of the 2011 donation.

One should not attribute too much significance to the Canadian/U.S. comparisons, as there are several plausible explanations for the large discrepancy in the size of charitable giving between the two countries. However, Canadians should definitely be mindful of the reality that Americans tend to contribute more to charity—measured as percentage of the population who give, percentage of income, or size of the contribution. Inasmuch as many Canadians view the American system as one of self-centered individualism, these facts should open minds up to the possibilities of *private* solutions to genuine public problems, such as alleviating the plight of the poor. Altruism comes in many forms; a society's compassion for the less fortunate should not be measured exclusively by the amount that government spends on relief programs.

Category 2: Myths based on conceptual mistakes

Economic Myth #10

There are market failures, but not government failures

One of the most common ways to justify government intervention in a particular industry or area of life is to point to a "market failure," a situation in which the profit-and-loss mechanism leads to an undesirable outcome. Scholars—especially those with a predisposition for more intervention—have identified scores of market failures. They have identified "negative externalities" in which the parties to a transaction impose harms on other people and thereby engage in too much of the activity. Examples would include carbon dioxide emissions leading to climate change damages, and cigarette consumption leading to higher health care costs. A standard solution for negative externalities is to impose a tax (on carbon content and cigarette purchases, in our examples) to cause people to "internalize the externality" and move behaviour in the "right" direction.

The market failure literature also includes cases of "positive externalities," in which the parties to a transaction impose benefits on other people and thereby engage in too little of the activity. For example, if decisions related to education were left purely to the private sector, students would largely consider the costs and benefits *to themselves* of paying for education, and would not end up buying the socially optimal amount. The standard solution for a positive externality is to enact a government subsidy, once again to move behaviour in the right direction.

Another textbook case of market failure is a so-called "public good," which (once produced) can be enjoyed by multiple people without diminishing its value, and from which it would be difficult to exclude non-customers of its enjoyment. Standard examples of a public good would be a lighthouse and nuclear deterrent against foreign missile attacks. Yes—the argument goes—in principle the private market could provide these items, but they wouldn't be produced in adequate amounts. Once a lighthouse is built, every ship captain can "free ride" off of its services. And even if everyone in the country would gladly pay his or share in order to build an adequate defense against foreign nuclear attacks, it would be a transactional nightmare for a private company to solicit individual payments to provide a service that would protect every Canadian, whether or not the person had contributed. Thus, it is standard to argue that public goods must be provided by government.

As the examples above illustrate, the concept of market failure can be applied quite liberally, since just about *every* activity could be construed as having externalities of one kind or another, and there are many items (scientific research, public parks, crime prevention, etc.) that have public-goods qualities. If all one does is focus on the failure of the market, candidates for government intervention will multiply like mushrooms after a rainstorm.

However, this attitude is what Harold Demsetz (1969) dubbed the "nirvana approach," in which we think of all the ways the market could systematically fail, while simply assuming that government officials will be exempt from any such inadequacies of their own.

In fact, there are several reasons to assume that *institutionally* government provision of services will be at a disadvantage compared to decentralized markets. For example, the ultimate policymakers (at least in a democratic society) are chosen by periodic elections, and they have authority over many different issues. If citizens don't like the phone service they receive from their local utility, they are unlikely to cast their vote in the next mayoral election on the basis of this single complaint, because there are so many other issues more important to them (taxes, crime, education, etc.). In contrast, if there are competing phone companies, then unhappy customers can quickly switch, providing targeted and immediate feedback to the underperforming firm. Consequently, there is much greater pressure to keep customers happy in decentralized, competitive markets than in a market with a government-granted monopoly.

The different institutional arrangement also explains why government agencies typically spend more money and achieve worse results, compared to a private company operating in a comparable industry. The head of a government agency has every incentive to *spend* his or her allotted budget, lest it be cut in the next round of fiscal decisions; there is a "use it or lose it" mentality. Furthermore, a mark of prestige among government agencies is the size of their employment. Worst of all, when a government agency fails in its ostensible purpose—such as inspecting food purity or airline safety—the knee-jerk reaction is to call for *more* funding and staff. These are undeniable features of government agencies in Canada (and other Western nations), yet they provide perverse incentives for bloated budgets and poor quality of service.

These worries are not merely hypothetical. In a 2013 report for the Fraser Institute, Lammam, MacIntyre, Clemens, Palacios, and Veldhuis reviewed the Canadian Auditor General's reports from the period 1988-2013, documenting many cases of *government* (as opposed to market) failure. To review some of the examples:

- The Canadian International Development Agency's (CIDA) development aid was often ineffective in helping the poor in developing countries, the ostensible purpose of the aid. For example, much of the $1.3 billion in relief aid given to Pakistan during the 1980s actually went to state-owned infrastructure projects rather than to programs that directly help the poorest citizens.

- In 1994, the Auditor General audit found that the number of escapes from minimum-security prisons increased 80% (from 112 to 202 escapes) from 1988-89 to 1993-94. During the period from April 1992 to March 1994, 390 prisoners escaped, and 28 of them committed serious offences while at large.

- In 1994, the Auditor General concluded that the trades-people within the DND were 33% less productive compared to commercial counterparts, costing taxpayers $50 million a year.

- Industry Canada sponsored the construction of a new fish plant in Quebec in 1986, which cost $2.2 million, even though at the time there was a federal moratorium on increasing fish-processing capacity. Supporters claimed that 250 jobs would be created by the new plant, but the Auditor General (in 1995) found that the new plant simply led to the closing of a nearby, already operating fish plant, which had as many employees as the new one.

- In 1997, the Auditor General found that the balances on public servants' credit cards (which had been issued to reduce reimbursement costs) had not been paid on time and led to $80,000 in unnecessary interest expenses for the government in a four-month period.

- In 1997, the Auditor General checked on the program in which Foreign Affairs officials receive additional housing benefits based on their hospitality expenses. Only four of the 43 cases examined actually met the department's own guidelines, and in one case an official received more than $32,000 in benefits even though the property had not been used for hospitality in four years.

- In 1998, the Auditor General reported that there were 3.8 million more Social Insurance Numbers (SINs) for Canadians aged 20 years and older than there were people in that age group, and more than half of SINs had no supporting documentation.

- In 2002, the Auditor General reported that the DND had taken eight years and spent $174 million developing a satellite communications system, but then determined that its existing commercial system was sufficient; the new system remains in storage.

- The government spent $508 million in 2000 on "cultural heritage," yet the Auditor General reported in 2003 that more than 90% of National Library collections are housed in buildings that "do not meet current standards for temperature and humidity."

- CIDA was unable to spend all of its initial tsunami funds (to relieve the disaster in Southern Asia) before the end of fiscal year 2004-05, and consequently spent the balance of $69 million on non-tsunami-related activities to free up funding for the new fiscal year.

- The Auditor General found in 2011 that the Canada Border Services Agency was failing to properly conduct security screens for visa applications. For example, 80% of the reviewed security screenings for permanent residence visas did not complete all the mandatory security checks.

- There was inadequate transparency in the $50 million G8 Legacy Infrastructure Fund, established to support the 2010 G8 Summit. For example, no documentation exists on how the 32 approved infrastructure projects were selected, and there were no consultations with Foreign Affairs (as required). In one case, a $9.75 million facility expansion project was not used for the purpose originally intended.

- In 2011-12, Human Resources and Skills Development Canada (HRSDC) made an estimated $578 million in undetected Employment Insurance overpayments, while it wrote off $62 million in unrecovered detected overpayments, penalties, and interest.

Anyone familiar with government operations will not be surprised by the above anecdotes. They are not intended as an indictment of Canadian government specifically, as they are symptomatic of the institutional, bureaucratic, and often-unaccountable nature of modern, democratic political systems throughout the Western world. What is intended by these examples is that we must always be mindful of *government failures* before rushing to recommend government solutions to perceived *market* failures.[54] As Nobel laureate economist George Stigler (1975) once remarked: "We may tell the society to jump out of the market frying pan, but we have no basis for predicting whether it will land in the fire or a luxurious bed."

---

54 See Carden and Horwitz (2013).

Economic Myth #11

The cost of government is the dollar amount of tax revenue it collects

When discussing a new tax increase, the media will often discuss the measure in terms of the projected revenue it will bring in over the years. For example, to describe a proposal as a "$10 billion tax hike" means that government revenues will be $10 billion higher than would otherwise be the case, because of the proposed policy change.

This common way of discussing tax policy is unfortunate, for it grossly *understates* the actual burden of taxation. For one thing, businesses and individuals must spend countless dollars and hours of time *complying* with the tax code—hiring tax attorneys and CPAs, saving receipts, filling out forms, and so forth.

Furthermore, the tax code is poorly designed from an efficiency standpoint, because it distorts the price incentives in the market and causes people to alter their behaviour in undesirable ways. For example, taxes on labour income reduce the incentive to work, while taxes on interest, dividends, and capital gains reduce the incentive to invest. These types of income taxes, therefore, reduce the total amount of output and growth from society's available resources, leaving many win-win transactions "on the table" because the tax code distorts the benefits reaped by the individuals involved. Thus, beyond the sheer dollar amount of revenue that is transferred from taxpayer to tax collector, the tax code carries with it an "excess burden" that makes society that much poorer.

Before walking through the specifics and giving numerical estimates of the Canadian tax code's excess burden on society, let's illustrate the concept with an exaggerated example. Suppose the government passes a new law imposing a $100 tax on every gallon of skim milk sold in the country. This outrageously high levy presumably would reduce the amount of skim milk sold to virtually zero, as people who originally bought it would switch to 1% milk (or whatever the lowest concentration of milkfat was legally allowed, to avoid the scope of the tax on "skim" milk). Now, because the gallons sold (at least officially) of skim milk would have collapsed to virtually nothing, the government would collect virtually no revenue from this new tax. Yet clearly it would be economically burdensome, as producers and consumers would have to adjust to an economy that no longer produced skim milk. This simple example, exaggerated though it is, underscores the important point that the burden of a tax is *not* simply the revenue flowing from taxpayers to the government.

Scholars with the Fraser Institute have engaged in an ongoing project to estimate the time, effort, and monetary expenses involved in tax compliance for both individuals and businesses.[55] They found that the compliance costs in 2011 for personal income taxes (at the federal, provincial, and municipal levels) were between $4.6 billion and $6.7 billion, for personal property taxes between $138.6 million and $246.2 million, and for business taxes between $14.5 billion and $17.8 billion. The authors noted that while the absolute dollar figure for compliance costs was higher for middle- and upper-income households and for large businesses, as a share of income (or revenue) compliance costs hit the lower-income and small- to mid-sized businesses hardest.

Adding the above components, the total estimated compliance costs to Canadian households and businesses from the tax code in 2011 ranged between $19.2 billion and $24.8 billion, or a whopping 1.1% to 1.4% of GDP. To reiterate, these figures represent just one particular aspect of the total burden of Canadian taxation, as these numbers reflect the amount of economic activity devoted merely to *complying with* (not paying) taxes.

In addition to estimating compliance costs borne by the taxpayer, the study also estimated the government's expenses in simply administering the

---

55 The latest estimates are provided in François Vaillancourt, Édison Roy-César, and Maria Silvia Barros (2013). *The Compliance and Administrative Costs of Taxation in Canada*. Fraser Institute.

tax code, which includes the maintenance of records and managing appeals. In 2011, this tax administration cost (including federal, provincial, and municipal levels) was estimated at $6.6 billion.

A separate Fraser research paper discussed not only the explicit compliance and administrative costs of Canadian taxes, but also the harmful effect on incentives of various types of taxes by listing their "marginal efficiency cost" (MEC).[56] The intuition for this concept is that not all taxes are created equal: To raise, say, $1 million in government revenue from a tax on income is more economically harmful than raising $1 million from a tax on consumption. Both options reduce the incentive to work and consume (because the whole point of earning income is to eventually spend it on consumption), but the tax on income introduces a *further* distortion by penalizing saving (because interest and dividend income is subject to the income tax). Thus, an income tax has a higher MEC than a consumption tax; society forfeits more potential economic output when the government raises $1 million from levying income taxes rather than consumption taxes. Relying on federal Department of Finance calculations, the authors report the estimated MEC for various Canadian taxes as of 1997 as summarized in **Table 3.6**.

Table 3.6: Estimates of Marginal Efficiency Costs (MEC) for select Canadian taxes

	MEC ($CDN)
Corporate income tax	$1.55
Personal income tax	$0.56
Payroll tax	$0.27
Sales tax	$0.17

Source: Clemens, Veldhuis, and Palacios, 2007: Table 1.

---

56 Jason Clemens, Niels Veldhuis, and Milagros Palacios (2007). *Tax Efficiency: Not All Taxes Are Created Equal.* Fraser Institute.

Table 3.6 illustrates what this section has discussed—namely that not all taxes are created equal. If the government raises an additional $1 million in revenue from corporate income taxes, the taxpayers not only pay the $1 million to the government, but economic output is $1,550,000 lower than it otherwise would have been, simply because of the effect on incentives from the higher rates levied on corporate earnings. In contrast, had the government raised the desired $1 million in additional revenue through a higher sales tax, then the economy would only be $170,000 smaller.

To be clear, these MEC figures refer merely to the (opportunity) *costs* of tax collection; they ignore the possible *benefits* of government spending of tax receipts. Yet regardless of the possible benefits of spending the money, policymakers should try to raise the funds in the least distortionary manner possible. For example, even if it were true that the government could still confer net benefits on society by raising $1 million via corporate income taxes and spending the revenue on an extremely important project that could not be achieved by the private market, there would be an opportunity for the government to deliver even *more* net benefits by switching to taxes with lower MECs.

When it comes to tax design, efficiency is not the *only* criterion, but it is an important one. The public and policymakers alike need to realize that the true cost of taxation is not merely the dollar amount of revenue flowing to the government, but also includes compliance and administrative costs, as well as the lost output due to distorted incentives.

Economic Myth #12

The success of an economic event is measured by how many jobs it creates

Especially during times of mass unemployment, it is typical to praise a government program or even a private-sector initiative because it "creates jobs." Judging from the public discourse, one might conclude that the purpose or function of companies is to provide jobs for their employees.

Yet this is fundamentally wrong. Broadly speaking, firms exist in order to efficiently transform scarce resources into valuable goods and services for their customers. To do this, of course, they incidentally "create jobs" for workers, just as they "create jobs" for tractors, hammers, and iron ore, as well. But whether these jobs are socially useful, or a complete waste of precious resources (including labour power) depends on the value of the *output* they produce.

For example, consider Project A, in which a firm hires 1,000 workers to build a bridge. Now consider Project B, in which a firm hires 2,000 workers to first build a bridge, then to knock it down. Project B "created more jobs" than Project A, yet there is an obvious sense in which Project A is more socially useful.

In fact, we can go so far as to say that an economic event is more successful if it takes *fewer* workers to achieve its results. The more that a project can economize on labour, without sacrificing the quality or quantity of its output, the more efficient it is. Society becomes richer, because now those workers are freed up to do other tasks, or to enjoy more leisure. Although these statements may sound paradoxical at first, a few examples should clarify.

First, consider health care and social assistance, an industry that had total employment of 1.7 million in Canada in 2012.[57] If there were a major medical breakthrough, such that a small and inexpensive device could cure virtually any illness, many of these 1.7 million Canadians would be thrown out of their jobs. Yet hardly a cause for dismay, this development would be one the greatest advances in recorded history. Yes, there would be financial hardship for, say, the young people just graduating medical school on the eve

---

57 Statistics Canada, CANSIM Table 281-0024.

of the scientific breakthrough; they would have trained for years, developing their minds and bodies for an occupation that no longer was needed. But it would make no sense to continue training some of society's sharpest minds and steadiest hands to become heart surgeons, if no patients ever needed heart surgery anymore.

Although our medical example is admittedly farfetched, a more realistic process occurs over the course of decades in a normal market economy, as technological advances and capital accumulation cause worker productivity to increase. Using more and more tools and machinery, a given worker is able to produce more and more output, so that the total number of workers in an industry may decline. Such a transformation may seem very unsettling and unfair to the displaced workers, but the shift is an undeniable boon to society as a whole.

Consider agriculture. Total male Canadian employment (age 15 and older) in this sector was 709,000 in the year 1891, but that figure had dropped to 405,000 by the year 1971 and was down to 215,500 by 2011.[58] Needless to say, even though total employment in Canada's agricultural sector declined sharply over the decades, agricultural *output* increased, often by a large factor for particular commodities.

Figure 3.13 summarizes some of the statistics. The story it presents is a common one: In an advancing market economy, entrepreneurs are constantly devising ways to achieve more with less, since that is the source of their profits. So long as there is a smoothly functioning labour market, the workers who are forced to leave sectors with shrinking employment are now available to fill other niches, which were previously unable to be filled. There aren't a fixed number of jobs in the economy; a "job" is created whenever two people—one with money and one with free time—have a similar vision and engage in a mutually advantageous deal.

Consider that in 2012, Canada had 798,000 people employed in professional, scientific, and technical services.[59] If the same proportion of the workforce had been devoted to agriculture as in 1891, there wouldn't have

---

58 Statistics Canada, Table M67-77 and CANSIM Table 282-0008. Note that there are slight differences in methodology in computing the relevant employment numbers over such a large time span, but the general trend—a rapid decline in agricultural employment in Canada—is clear enough.

59 Statistics Canada, CANSIM Table 281-0024.

Figure 3.13: Total male employment and selected output in agriculture, 1891–2012 (selected years)

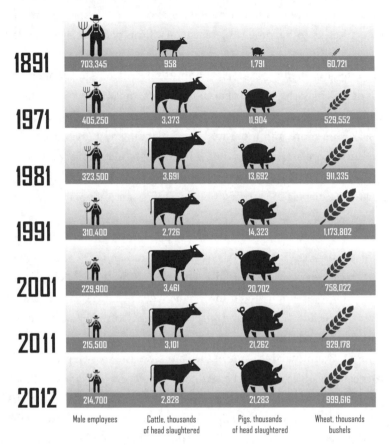

	Male employees	Cattle, thousands of head slaughtered	Pigs, thousands of head slaughtered	Wheat, thousands bushels
1891	703,345	958	1,791	60,721
1971	405,250	3,373	11,904	529,552
1981	323,500	3,691	13,692	911,335
1991	310,400	2,726	14,323	1,173,802
2001	229,900	3,461	20,702	758,022
2011	215,500	3,101	21,262	929,178
2012	214,700	2,828	21,283	999,616

Sources: Statistics Canada, 1999; Statistics Canada CANSIM Tables 282-0008, 001-0017, 003-0026, 003-0028.

been enough people available to fill so many technical jobs. (Plus, with the enhanced productivity of farm labour, Canadians would be overrun with wheat and hogs if they retained such high levels of agricultural employment.)

It's true that workers often take great pride in their labour, and that modern citizens often derive their sense of self-esteem from their employment. In light of these considerations, it still might seem that "creating jobs" is a useful task for government policymakers. However, using a simple household analogy helps us see the real problems with government trying to take on the role of job creator. Many people want to be "productive" around the house, and would feel miserable if they wasted the entire weekend watching television or sleeping. Yet even among these people, they would use their time as *efficiently* as possible. The goal wouldn't be "to keep busy" or "give myself work," but rather the goal would be *to get things done*. Someone who wants to paint a bedroom will use a paintbrush or a roller, rather than a toothbrush. Someone who wants to cut the grass will use a mower, rather than a scissors. Thus, we see that even among people who want to "stay busy" and avoid sloth, the actual objective isn't work per se—it's *productive and useful* work. If a person can knock out a given chore with less labour time by using tools and equipment, that's great; it means the person can then use his freed-up labour to accomplish *more* chores during the weekend.

The same is true when it comes to the labour market in the aggregate. Even though there are emotional, social, and cultural considerations tied to employment, ultimately it makes no sense—and shouldn't boost anyone's morale—to have workers perform useless tasks, or to perform useful tasks but in an inefficient manner. Yes, government policymakers could "create jobs" by insisting that road crews use mules, rather than trucks, but such a procedure would be patently absurd. Although the principle is obvious enough in this exaggerated example, very often in modern policy debates, proponents will champion a particular government measure—even though it fails the profit and loss test—because it "creates jobs." As we've demonstrated above, the fact that a project requires the use of scarce labour is actually a strike *against* it, other things equal.

Economic Myth #13

Canada suffers from a "resource curse"

Many high-profile Canadians—including the former Premier of Ontario, Dalton McGuinty, and the Leader of the Official Opposition (NDP), Thomas Mulcair—have claimed that the country suffers from an alleged "resource curse." The concept is sometimes called the "Dutch disease," in reference to the experience in the Netherlands in the 1970s. In a nutshell, the allegation is that during times of high worldwide commodity prices, resource-rich countries (including Canada) will see a strengthening of their currencies as other countries must pay more for their imports of oil, natural gas, and other commodities. The strong currencies then make it difficult for the manufacturers in the resource-rich countries to export *their* wares, so that effectively the countries specialize in shipping out "stuff in the ground" instead of *making* goods and services with their skilled workers.

There are several problems with this typical "resource curse" argument, both logical and empirical.[60] Before even looking at the data, we can ask: Do the critics agree that the world is better off because these resources exist in the first place? In other words, surely the critics agree that humans as a whole are richer because the planet has been endowed with large quantities of commodities, rather than humanity finding itself on a barren rock.

Now, given that we agree these resources should exist, the next question is: Would the critics prefer that the resources be distributed within or beyond Canada's borders? In other words, would the critics prefer that Canada's rich mineral deposits be magically transported to *other* countries, so that *their* citizens could sell them to others for a perpetual flow of goods and financial assets?

These questions should hopefully underscore that the "resource curse" argument doesn't add up.[61] Part of the problem is that it views the development

---

60 The discussion for this first myth closely follows Robert P. Murphy and Brian Lee Crowley (2012). *No Dutch Treat: Oil and Gas Wealth Benefits All of Canada*. MLI Commentary (May).

61 It is possible to argue that in countries with politically unstable regimes, the presence of abundant natural resources (such as oil) that can be easily exported, allows the perpetuation of the ruling regime, and in that sense could be construed as a "curse." However, in the text we are addressing the more narrow economic claim—the one relevant for Canada—that natural resources can alter trade flows and thus directly hurt the economic interests of the country.

of mineral resources (such as oil and gas) as somehow less truly "productive" than the production of manufactured goods. Yet this is a spurious objection, because in the grand scheme *nobody* in private enterprise produces anything from scratch; even farmers "merely" rearrange the materials that nature has already given us. It takes skilled workers, operating specially designed equipment and machinery, to efficiently extract oil and gas, and to deliver them to other firms that will refine them for use by the ultimate consumer. This is just as surely "production" as skilled workers, operating specially designed equipment and machinery, assembling components into a jet aircraft.

Another problem with the "resource curse" argument is that it ignores how the *exporting regions* spend the money they receive. Yes, it is true that (other things equal) a stronger Canadian dollar means that manufacturers in, say, Ontario will have a harder time selling their goods to foreigners. But if the Canadian dollar is strong because of high world oil prices, then Canadians in, say, Alberta will be that much richer, and have that much more to spend on Ontario-produced items.

There have been empirical estimates of this type of effect. For example, the Canadian Energy Research Institute (CERI) published a study in 2009 of the economic impact, broken down at the provincial level, from various elements of the petroleum sector.[62] Specifically, the 2009 CERI report analyzed economic impacts on specific types of energy, in specific provinces and territories:

> Alberta (conventional oil, conventional gas, CBM, oil sands, major capital projects), British Columbia (conventional oil, conventional gas, shale/tight gas, major capital projects), Saskatchewan (conventional oil, conventional gas), Manitoba (conventional oil), Quebec (major capital projects), Nova Scotia (conventional gas) and Northwest Territories (major capital projects). Due to insufficient data analysis was not possible for several sources of energy, such as the Oil Sands in Saskatchewan or the large potential of the shale gas plays in Quebec.[63]

---

62 Canadian Energy Research Institute [CERI] (2009). *Economic Impacts of the Petroleum Industry in Canada: Summary Report*. CERI.

63 Canadian Energy Research Institute: 2.

The results of the study are presented in **Table 3.8**, which provides a wealth of information, once one understands its layout. Each column represents the economic impact generated across all provinces by petroleum industry activities within that particular column's province. For example, looking at the second column "BC" and moving down, we see that over the twenty-five-year period specified (2008-2033), petroleum activities in British Columbia will generate an estimated $13.0 billion in additional output in Alberta, $376.1 billion in British Columbia itself, $1.9 billion in Manitoba, and so on. (Note that these figures are simple summations, not discounted present values.) In the same column, we see that Alberta petroleum operations also generate $36.7 billion in additional output in Quebec.

On the other hand, if we want to see the total impact on output that the petroleum industry has for the province of Ontario, we would look at the "ON" row (ninth from the top) in Table 3.8. The petroleum sector's operations in Alberta alone generate $116.2 billion in output in Ontario, British Columbia generates $12.4 billion, and so on, for a total impact of $149.1 billion in Ontario.

Table 3.8: CERI (2009) model's estimate of total impact on provincial GDP from petroleum industry, 2008 $ million, 2008–2033

	AB	BC	MB	NT	NS	QC	SK	Total
AB	2,530,656	13,036	346	1,753	351	44	14,305	2,560,491
BC	93,093	376,078	271	1,603	255	45	7,557	478,903
MB	18,705	1,901	10,152	462	17	15	5,611	36,863
NB	3,634	599	27	115	69	20	374	4,839
NL	3,390	371	19	95	59	10	280	4,224
NT	2,650	230	6	17,146	111	1	204	20,348
NS	5,903	824	29	192	6,146	18	433	13,544
NU	572	57	2	406	2	1	34	1,073
ON	116,168	12,432	612	3,010	320	228	16,369	149,140
PE	736	118	5	30	32	3	64	987
QC	36,652	5,934	277	1,163	122	1,640	3,178	48,966
SK	44,346	2,528	173	478	37	12	198,305	245,879
YT	672	211	2	29	1	-	33	948
Total	2,857,178	414,318	11,920	26,483	7,522	2,038	246,747	3,566,206

Sources: Adapted from CERI, 2009. Some totals appear slightly incorrect due to rounding.

As these data indicate, the petroleum industry generates substantial economic activity not just in the oil-rich provinces, but in *all* of Canada. After all, extraction operations in Alberta will drive the demand for construction equipment produced in Ontario (and elsewhere). On both theoretical and empirical grounds, therefore, we can reject the myth that Canada suffers from a "resource curse." Canadians should be grateful for their rich natural heritage, and should expect policymakers to make decisions to foster the best use of all resources, whether natural, labour, or physical capital.

Economic Myth #14

Only the government can redistribute income, or provide public goods

In Myth #3, we pointed out that governments can fail (just as the critics like to harp on market failures), and we listed numerous examples from recent Canadian history. Yet a related myth is that only government is capable of achieving certain "social" goals, such as providing a more equitable income distribution or producing so-called public goods. On the contrary, free citizens in a market economy are perfectly capable of deviating from narrow "bottom line" decision-making, and can use their wealth and time for non-pecuniary ends.

The most obvious example of extra-governmental philanthropy is direct charitable giving, a topic we cover in detail above (in Myth #13). Yet there are entire organizations dedicated to ends that some people consider the exclusive realm of government action. Consider, for example, the Canadian branch of the Red Cross. According to its 2012-13 annual report,[64] the Canadian Red Cross:

* Provided First Aid and water safety training courses to 1.7 million Canadians, with 23,000 active instructors.

* Served 145,175 clients in health and social programs, providing more than 3 million client service-hours.

---

64 See <http://www.redcross.ca/crc/documents/Who-We-Are/Red-Cross-AR-2013-e.pdf>.

- Provided almost 270,000 rides through its transportation programs.

- Provided almost 225,000 meals through the "Meals on Wheels" program.

- Channeled more than $14 million in global emergency response assistance to crises around the world, with 49 emergency relief and recovery operations in 37 countries.

- Enabled volunteers in Canada to donate more than 65,000 hours to disaster relief efforts.

Consider another non-profit organization: Little League Baseball Canada. According to its website,[65] it only has two full-time employees, and yet more than 35,000 Canadian children (along with 100,000 parents and other supporters) participate.

Naturally, hockey is a much more popular sport than baseball here in Canada. According to its website,[66] Hockey Canada in 2012-13 registered more than 537,000 male and almost 87,000 female players. Minor hockey in Canada is obviously a massive undertaking, with thousands of coaches and officials, and which seeks to not merely provide entertainment for spectators but to instill skill, respect, and sportsmanship among the players. Canadians just take the existence of such a coordinated enterprise for granted, but this is clearly not something that needs to be designed and maintained by the government; minor hockey leagues show that free citizens in a market economy have the wealth and spare time to develop all sorts of "extra market" activities.

More generally, Canadian society is full of non-profit organizations. As of December 2013 the Canadian Revenue Agency documents more than 86,000 registered charities alone (which are just a subset of non-profit organizations).[67]

---

65 See <http://www.littleleague.ca/english/about/>.

66 See <http://www.hockeycanada.ca/en-ca/Corporate/About/Basics/Registration>.

67 The tally of registered charities can be seen by entering the somewhat cumbersome URL: <http://www.cra-arc.gc.ca/ebci/haip/srch/advancedsearchresult-eng.action?n=&b=&q=&s=registered&d=&e=+&c=&v=+&o=&z=&g=+&t=+&y=+&p=1>.

Conceptually, there is a certain tension in the popular (but misguided) notion that it requires the coercive hand of *government* to undertake activities—such as donating the community's excess wealth to relieve poverty or aid in disaster relief, or to promote literacy and vaccination—that just about all civilized people support. Consider: The more "obvious" and nearly universal the public support for a particular program, the easier it should be to provide voluntarily outside the sphere of government. On the other hand, if a particular program does *not* command widespread support, such that it could only exist if propped up with tax dollars and/or government regulations, then it raises the question of whether a large proportion of the citizenry should be *forced* to fund a project with which they disagree?

These reflections do not definitively settle the question of which programs belong in the sphere of government provision, and which should be left to either the for-profit market or the voluntary non-profit sphere, but we *have* shown that government provision should not be a default. Even if Canadians agree that a particular program or goal is a worthwhile endeavor, it doesn't automatically follow that it therefore is a candidate for government provision. Proponents must further explain why it makes sense to forcibly extract resources from Canadian citizens (through taxation and regulations) if Canadian citizens will not support the program voluntarily with their time and money.

As a concluding remark on this myth, we must also remember that the current provision of charitable donations—voluntary "income redistribution"—and other civic-minded activities is done *in the presence of* large taxation and government spending on these same types of programs. Canadians would presumably donate a larger fraction of their income (and volunteer more of their time) if their tax burden were lower, and if they realized that the government wouldn't be there to "solve" a particular social problem or issue. It is important to remember that the government does not create resources of its own; when people say that the government ought to "do something" about a particular problem, to be successful it must take the necessary resources away from the private sector. To justify such actions, proponents must offer a compelling reason why voluntary action cannot mobilize the same resources as effectively as government officials.

Economic Myth #15

Government-owned and operated services save money for consumers because they eliminate the middleman's markup, allowing for lower prices

It is a common myth that governments can deliver a given service very cheaply—"at cost"—whereas private delivery requires a "mark up" above the cost to give the private investors a return on their capital. Since the private business owners are in it for profit, whereas the government managers are interested only in serving the public, it seems only natural to conclude that government ownership leads to leaner enterprises and lower prices.

Framing the issue in this (typical) way ignores the opportunity cost of the government's funds. For example, suppose there is a construction project that requires $1 million in upfront direct expenditure (on real estate, workers, lumber, glass, etc.), and which will be ready for sale in one year's time. A private developer, it's true, will *not* want to invest that money in order to then sell the finished project for $1 million. Instead, he will only undertake the project if he thinks he will be able to sell it for, say, $1.1 million, thus earning a 10% return on his one-year investment of capital.

In contrast, a government-owned enterprise could spend the same $1 million to finance the project, and then sell it (one year later) "at cost" for $1 million, avoiding any mark up. But in reality, this would be selling the finished project for *below* cost, because the $1 million that was tied up for a year in the construction project could have instead been used to retire $1 million of the government's outstanding debt. If the yield on government bonds is 5%, that represents an opportunity cost of $50,000 in extra interest payments that the taxpayers must make, because of the decision to finance the project and then sell it "at cost."

At this point, the case for government enterprises has been knocked down to a *difference* in yields—the return desired by the private investor (10% in our example), versus the interest rate on government bonds (5% in our example). Yet even this slimmer advantage further erodes when we ponder *why it is* that the return on government debt is typically lower than on other investments: uncertainty. The *reason* private investors typically insist on a higher rate of return ("profit margin") than the government must pay to borrow money, is that investment projects are less likely to pay off than the government's ability to extract interest payments from the taxpayers.

The upshot of these considerations is that even if it were true that the government could enter an industry and "save citizens money" by providing services at lower prices than would be possible with private ownership, this outcome would not necessarily be benign. It would at least partially reflect the fact that the government managers were putting taxpayers on the hook for a risky investment on terms that nobody in the private sector would be willing to accept with his own money on the line. The future is not certain. If the government effectively acts as a hedge fund manager—using the taxpayers as investors—and doesn't even attempt to earn a decent rate of return (charging "above cost") on its collection of projects, then it is guaranteeing that the taxpayers will eventually lose money. Thus the taxpayers suffer investment losses (on the projects that turn out to be a waste of resources) that counterbalance their supposed gains as customers of the services provided "at cost" by the government.

Yet there is another, even more fundamental problem with the typical claim that government-operated services save money for customers. Namely, "the cost" of providing a particular service is *not* an objective fact of the world, analogous to the boiling point of water. In reality, business owners must *discover* the least-cost way of providing a good or service to their customers. Both theory and history show that a competitive industry, with firms owned by private individuals who will directly benefit from any profits, is more likely to spawn such cost-cutting discoveries than a monopolized industry with a single government producer.

This outcome is not due to maliciousness or incompetence on the part of the monopoly producer, but reflects the different institutional structure: An entrenched government enterprise has less incentive to experiment with new methods of production in order to lower costs, because it has a captive market and the people responsible for the innovations will not personally pocket the savings (the way private owners do). In addition, a government-owned enterprise will likely be more susceptible to political forces, for example, relying more heavily on labour than on physical capital.

The empirical evidence supports this reasoning. In a Fraser Institute report, Veldhuis, Palacios, Lammam, and Gainer (2009) summarize some of the key findings in the literature. For example, William Megginson and colleagues (1994) looked at 61 government-business enterprises (GBEs) in 18 countries and 32 industries that were privatized during the period 1961–1990. They found that profitability soared by 45%, efficiency rose by 11%, output increased by 27%, and capital investment increased 44%. A later, more comprehensive study in 2001 by Megginson and Jeffry Netter reviewed the academic literature on privatization and led the authors to conclude that "privatization 'works,' in the sense that divested firms almost always become more efficient, more profitable, and financially healthier, and increase their capital investment spending."[68]

---

68 William L. Megginson and Jeffry M. Netter (2001). From State to Market: A Survey of Empirical Studies on Privatization. *Journal of Economic Literature* 39, 2: 281.

Works cited

Angevine, Gerry, and Graham Thomson (2008). *Eliminating Barriers to Worker Mobility: Increasing the Availability of Skilled Labor in Alberta's Oil Sands Industry*. Fraser Alert (July). Fraser Institute.

Bastiat, Frédéric (1850 [1996]). *Economic Harmonies*. George B. de Huszar (trans.). W. Hayden Boyers (ed.). Library of Economics and Liberty.

Bergh, Andreas and Martin Karlsson (2010). Government Size and Growth: Accounting for Economic Freedom and Globalization. *Public Choice* 142, 1–2: 195–213.

Bjornskov, Christian and Nicolai J. Foss (2008). Economic Freedom and Entrepreneurial Activity: Some Cross-Country Evidence. *Public Choice* 134, 3–4 (March): 307–328.

Block, Walter E. (1990). *Economics and the Environment: A Reconciliation*. Fraser Institute.

Block, Walter E. (1990). Environmental Problems, Private Property Rights Solutions. In Walter Block (ed.), *Economics and the Environment: A Reconciliation* (Fraser Institute): 281–318.

Carden, Art, and Steven Horwitz (2013, April 1). *Is Market Failure a Sufficient Condition for Government Intervention?* Library of Economics and Liberty.
<http://www.econlib.org/library/Columns/y2013/CardenHorwitzmarkets.html>

Chant, John F., Donald G. McFetridge, and Douglas A. Smith (1990). The Economics of the Conserver Society. In Walter E. Block (ed.), *Economics and the Environment: A Reconciliation*. Fraser Institute.

Chaussard, Martine, Megan Gerecke, and Jody Heymann (no date). *The Work Equity Canada Index: Where the Provinces and Territories Stand*. Institute for Health and Social Policy. McGill University. <http://www.mcgill.ca/ihsp/sites/mcgill.ca.ihsp/files/WorkEquityCanada.pdf>

Clemens, Jason, and Niels Veldhuis (2013). Hayekian Perspectives on Canada's Economic and Social Reforms of the 1990s. In Sandra J. Peart and David M. Levy (eds.), *F.A. Hayek and the Modern Economy: Economic Organization and Activity*. Palgrave Macmillan.

Clemens, Jason, Niels Veldhuis, and Milagros Palacios (2007). *Tax Efficiency: Not All Taxes Are Created Equal*. Studies in Economic Prosperity, No. 4 (January). Fraser Institute.

Davidson, Sinclair (2005). The 1997–98 Asian Crisis: A Property Rights Perspective. *Cato Journal* 25, 3 (Fall). <http://www.freetheworld.com/papers/1997-98-Asian-Crisis-A-Property-Rights-Perspective.pdf>

Demsetz, Harold (1969). Information and Efficiency: Another Viewpoint. *Journal of Law and Economics* 12, 1 (April): 1–22.

Emerson, J. W., A. Hsu, M. A. Levy, A. de Sherbinin, V. Mara, D. C. Esty, and M. Jaiteh (2012). *2012 Environmental Performance Index and Pilot Trend Environmental Performance Index*. Yale Center for Environmental Law and Policy. <http://epi.yale.edu/files/2012_epi_report.pdf>

Engen, Eric, and Jonathan Skinner (1996). Taxation and Economic Growth. *National Tax Journal*, 49, 4 (December): 617–42.

Esmail, Nadeem, and Michael Walker (2008). *How Good Is Canadian Health Care? 2008 Report: An International Comparison of Health Care Systems*. Studies in Health Care Policy (November). Fraser Institute.

Feldmann, Horst (2009a). The Quality of the Legal System and Labor Market Performance around the World. *European Journal of Law and Economics* 28, 1: 39–65.

Feldmann, Horst (2009b). Business Regulation, Labor Force Participation and Employment in Industrial Countries. *Journal of Economics and Business* 61, 3: 238–260.

Feldmann, Horst (2009c). The Unemployment Effects of Labor Regulation around the World. *Journal of Comparative Economics* 37, 1: 76–90.

Friedman, Milton and Rose Friedman. *Free to Choose: A Personal Statement*. Harcourt Inc.

Gay, Juan G., Valérie Paris, Marion Devaux, and Michael de Looper (2011). *Mortality Amenable to Health Care in 31 OECD Countries: Estimates and Methodological Issues*. OECD Health Working Papers, No. 55. OECD.

Globalization at the Crossroads (2014). *Bureaucracy and Corruption*. Web page. The Power of the Poor.
<http://www.thepowerofthepoor.com/concepts/c7.php>

Godin, Keith, and Niels Veldhuis (2009). *The Economic Effects of Increasing British Columbia's Minimum Wage*. Studies in Labour Markets. Fraser Institute.

Griswold, Daniel T. (2004). *Trading Tyranny for Freedom: How Open Markets Till the Soil for Democracy*. Trade Policy Analysis No. 26. Cato Institute (January). <http://www.cato.org/publications/trade-policy-analysis/trading-tyranny-freedom-how-open-markets-till-soil-democracy>

Gwartney, D. James, Randall G. Holcombe, and Robert A. Lawson (2006). Institutions and the Impact of Investment on Growth. *Kyklos* 59, 2: 255–273.

Hall, Joshua C., Russel S. Sobell, and George R. Crowley (2010). Institutions, Capital, and Growth. *Southern Economic Journal* 77, 2: 385–405.

Hazlitt, Henry (1946 [1979]). *Economics in One Lesson*. Crown Publishers.

Hill v. Nova Scotia (1997). Judgments of the Supreme Court of Canada. <http://scc.lexum.org/decisia-scc-csc/scc-csc/scc-csc/en/item/1466/index.do>

Horwitz, Steven. (2003). The Costs of Inflation Revisited. *The Review of Austrian Economics*, 16:1, 77–95.

Howard, Peter, Afshin Khademvatani, Paul Kralovic, David McColl, Melissa Mei, Abbas Naini, Rami Shabaneh, Asghar Shahmoradi, Martin Slagorsky, and Thorn Walden (2009). *Economic Impacts of the Petroleum Industry in Canada*. CERI Study No. 120, Summary Report (June). Canadian Energy Research Institute. <http://www.ceri.ca/docs/CERI10SummaryReport.pdf>

KPMG (2014). *Canadian Personal Tax Tables*. KPMG. <http://www.kpmg.com/ca/en/issuesandinsights/articlespublications/pages/taxratespersonal.aspx>

Lammam, Charles, Amela Karabegović, and Niels Veldhuis (2012). *Measuring Income Mobility in Canada*. Studies in Economic Prosperity (November). Fraser Institute. <http://www.fraserinstitute.org/uploadedFiles/fraser-ca/Content/research-news/research/publications/measuring-income-mobility-in-canada.pdf>

Lammam, Charles, Hugh MacIntyre, Jason Clemens, Milagros Palacios, and Niels Veldhuis (2013). *Federal Government Failure in Canada, 2013 Report: A Review of the Auditor General's Reports, 1988–2013*. Fraser Institute (October). <http://www.fraserinstitute.org/uploadedFiles/fraser-ca/Content/research-news/research/publications/federal-government-failure-in-canada-2013.pdf>

Lawhaha.com (2012, November 13). Warning: Canadian Coffee Seller Makes Fun of Hot Coffee Warnings. <http://lawhaha.com/warning-canadian-coffee-seller-makes-fun-of-hot-coffee-warnings/>

Lawson, Robert A. and J.R. Clark (2010). Examining the Hayek-Friedman Hypothesis on Economic and Political Freedom. *Journal of Economic Behavior & Organization* 74, 3 (June): 230–239.

Lee, Young, and Roger H. Gordon (2005). Tax Structure and Economic Growth. *Journal of Public Economics* 89, 5–6 (June): 1027–43.

Long, James (1999). Updated Estimates of the Wage Mobility of Minimum Wage Workers. *Journal of Labor Research* 20, 4 (Fall): 493–503.

Lothian, James R. (2006). Institutions, Capital Flows and Financial Integration. *Journal of International Money and Finance* 25, 1–12: 358–369.

MacIntyre, Hugh, and Charles Lammam (2013). *Generosity in Canada and the United States: The 2013 Generosity Index.* Research Bulletin (December). Fraser Institute. <http://www.fraserinstitute.org/uploadedFiles/fraser-ca/Content/research-news/research/publications/GenerosityIndex_2013.pdf>

Megginson, William L., Robert C. Nash, and Matthias Van Randenborgh (1994). The Financial and Operating Performance of Newly Privatized Firms: An International Empirical Analysis. *Journal of Finance* 49, 2 (June): 403–52.

Megginson, William L. and Jeffry M. Netter (2001). From State to Market: A Survey of Empirical Studies on Privatization. *Journal of Economic Literature* 39, 2: 321–89.

Milke, Mark (2013, February 9). Abolish the $3.6 Billion Tariff Tax on the Poor. *Calgary Herald.* <http://www.fraserinstitute.org/research-news/news/commentaries/Abolish-the-$3-6-billion-tariff-tax-on-the-poor/>

Mises, Ludwig von (1944). *Bureaucracy.* Ludwig von Mises Institute. <http://mises.org/etexts/mises/bureaucracy.asp>

Murphy, Robert P., and Brian Lee Crowley (2012). No Dutch Treat: Oil and Gas Wealth Benefits All of Canada. *MLI Commentary.* Macdonald-Laurier

Institute (May). <http://www.macdonaldlaurier.ca/files/pdf/Oil-and-gas-wealth-benefits-all-of-Canada-Commentary-May-2012.pdf>

New York Law School Center for Justice and Democracy (no date). *McDonalds' Hot Coffee Case—Read the Facts Not the Fiction.* Web page. Texas Trial Lawyers Association. <https://www.ttla.com/index.cfm?pg=McDonaldsCoffeeCaseFacts>

Offman, Craig (2008, February 7). Jail Politicians Who Ignore Climate Science: Suzuki. *National Post.* <http://www.nationalpost.com/news/story.html?id=290513>

Organisation for Economic Cooperation and Development [OECD] (2013a). *Health at a Glance 2013: OECD Indicators.* OECD Publishing. <http://www.oecd.org/els/health-systems/Health-at-a-Glance-2013.pdf>

Organisation for Economic Cooperation and Development [OECD] (2013b). *Education at a Glance 2013: OECD Indicators.* OECD Publishing. <http://www.oecd.org/edu/eag2013%20(eng)--FINAL%2020%20June%202013.pdf>

Palacios, Milagros, and Jason Clemens (2013). *Comparing Public and Private Sector Compensation in Canada.* Studies in Labour Markets (April). Fraser Institute. <http://www.fraserinstitute.org/uploadedFiles/fraser-ca/Content/research-news/research/publications/comparing-public-and-private-sector-compensation-in-canada.pdf>

Palda, Filip (1994). *Provincial Trade Wars: Why the Blockade Must End.* Fraser Institute.

Powell, Jim (2003). *FDR's Folly: How Roosevelt and His New Deal Prolonged the Great Depression.* Three Rivers Press.

Ray, Dixy Lee (1992). *Trashing the Planet: How Science Can Help Us Deal with Acid Rain, Depletion of the Ozone, and Nuclear Waste (Among Other Things).* Perennial.

Romer, Christina D., and David H. Romer (2010). The Macroeconomic Effects of Tax Changes: Estimates Based on a New Measure of Fiscal Shocks. *American Economic Review* 100, 3 (June): 763–801.

Roychoudhury, Saurav, and Robert A. Lawson (2010). Economic Freedom and Sovereign Credit Ratings and Default Risk. *Journal of Financial Economic Policy* 2, 2: pp. 149–162.

Schaefer, Brett D. (2005). Proposals for an Environmental Indicator for the MCA Should Be Resisted. *Heritage Backgrounder* #1896 (November 14). Heritage Foundation. <http://www.heritage.org/research/reports/2005/11/proposals-for-an-environmental-indicator-for-the-mca-should-be-resisted>

Science Council of Canada (1977). *Canada as Conserver Society: Resource Uncertainties and the Need for New Technologies.* Science Council of Canada.

Smith, Adam (1776). *An Inquiry into the Nature and Causes of the Wealth of Nations.*

Smith, Jessica (2013, March 11).Getting a Fare Deal: Why Toronto's Taxi Industry Is Failing, and What To Do about It. *Metro Toronto.* <http://metronews.ca/news/toronto/589821/why-torontos-taxi-industry-is-failing-and-what-to-do-about-it/>

Smith, Ralph, and Bruce Vavrichek (1992). The Wage Mobility of Minimum Wage Workers. *Industrial and Labor Relations Review* 46, 1: 82–88.

Soysa, Indra de, and Krishna Chaitanya Vadlammanati (2011). Do Pro-market Economic Reforms Drive Human Rights Violations? An Empirical Assessment, 1981 – 2006. *Public Choice,* 155 (2013): 163–187. <http://www.uni-heidelberg.de/md/awi/professuren/intwipol/public_choice.pdf>

Statistics Canada (1999). *Historical Statistics of Canada.* Catalogue No. 11-516-X. Section M: Agriculture. <http://www.statcan.gc.ca/pub/11-516-x/sectionm/4057754-eng.htm>

Statistics Canada (2010). *Minimum Wage. Perspectives on Labour and Income*. Catalogue no. 75-001-XIE. Statistics Canada.

Stigler, George (1975). The Economists' Traditional Theory of the Economic Functions of the State. *The Citizen and the State: Essays on Regulation* University of Chicago Press.

Stroup, Michael (2007). *The Influence of Capitalism and Democracy on Air Emissions among OECD Countries*. Working Paper.

Vaillancourt, François, Édison Roy-César, and Maria Silvia Barros (2013). *The Compliance and Administrative Costs of Taxation in Canada*. Studies in Tax Policy (April). Fraser Institute.

Valaskakis, Kimon, Peter Sindell, and J. Graham Smith (1977). *The Selective Conserver Society*. GAMMA.

Veldhuis, Niels, Milagros Palacios, Charles Lammam, and Alex Gainer (2009). *Saskatchewan Prosperity: Building on Success*. Studies in Economic Prosperity (February). Fraser Institute.

Waverman, Leonard (1991). A Canadian Vision of North American Economic Integration. In Steven Globerman (ed.), *Continental Accord: North American Economic Integration*. Fraser Institute.

Wilde, Gerald J.S. (2001). *Target Risk 2.* PDE Publications.

Wood, Joel (2013). *Canadian Environmental Indicators—Water*. Studies in Environmental Policy (July). Fraser Institute.

Wood, Joel (2012, July/August). Free Our Cities. *Fraser Forum*. <http://www.fraserinstitute.org/uploadedFiles/fraser-ca/Content/research-news/research/articles/regulation-review-free-our-cities.pdf>

Yandle, Bruce (1983). Bootleggers and Baptists: The Education of a Regulatory Economist. *Regulation* 7, 3: 12.

About the authors

Robert P. Murphy

Robert P. Murphy is a Fraser Institute Senior Fellow. He earned his PhD in economics from New York University. He taught for three years at Hillsdale College before entering the financial sector, working for Laffer Associates on research papers as well as portfolio management. Dr. Murphy is now the president of Consulting By RPM and runs the economics blog *Free Advice*. He has written several books, including *The Politically Incorrect Guide to Capitalism* (Regnery, 2007) and *Lessons for the Young Economist* (Mises Institute, 2010). He has also written hundreds of economics articles for the layperson, and has given numerous radio and television interviews on such outlets as Fox Business and CNBC.

Jason Clemens

Jason Clemens is the Fraser Institute's Executive Vice-President. He held a number of positions with the Fraser Institute between 1996 and 2008, including Director of Research Quality, Director of Budgeting and Strategic Planning, and Director of Fiscal Studies. He most recently worked with the Ottawa-based Macdonald-Laurier Institute (MLI) as Director of Research and held a similar position with the San Francisco-based Pacific Research Institute for over three years. Mr. Clemens has an Honours Bachelors Degree of Commerce and a Masters Degree in Business Administration from the University of Windsor as well as a Post-Baccalaureate Degree in Economics from Simon Fraser University. He has published over 70 major studies on a wide range of topics, including taxation, government spending, labour market regulation, banking, welfare reform, health care, productivity, and entrepreneurship. He has published nearly 300 shorter articles, which have appeared in such newspapers as the *Wall Street Journal, Investors' Business Daily, Washington Post, Globe and Mail, National Post*, and a host of other US, Canadian, and international newspapers. In 2012, the Governor General of Canada, on behalf of Her Majesty the Queen, presented Mr. Clemens with the Queen Elizabeth II Diamond Jubilee Medal in recognition of his contributions to the country.

Milagros Palacios

Milagros Palacios is a Senior Research Economist at the Fraser Institute. She holds a BA in Industrial Engineering from the Pontifical Catholic University of Peru and a M.Sc. in Economics from the University of Concepción, Chile. Since joining the Institute, she has published or co-published over 60 research studies and over 60 commentaries on a wide range of public policy issues including taxation, government finances, investment, productivity, labour markets, and charitable giving.

Niels Veldhuis

Niels Veldhuis is the President of the Fraser Institute. He has written six books and more than 50 comprehensive studies on a wide range of economic topics including taxation, banking, productivity, investment, entrepreneurship, labour markets, and government finances. His latest book, *The Canadian Century: Moving out of America's Shadow*, is a national bestseller published by Key Porter in May 2010. Mr. Veldhuis appears regularly on radio and television programs across Canada and the United States. He has written more than 200 commentaries that have appeared in over 50 newspapers including the *Globe and Mail*, *Wall Street Journal*, and *The Economist*. He holds a Bachelor degree in Business Administration and a Master degree in Economics from Simon Fraser University. In 2010, he was named one of Vancouver's Forty under 40 by *Business in Vancouver* and in 2011 led a discussion between former presidents Bill Clinton and George W. Bush at the Surrey Economic Forum.

Acknowledgments

The authors wish to thank the Lotte and John Hecht Memorial Foundation for their generous support of this project, and the many anonymous reviewers for their helpful comments and suggestions. Any errors, omissions, or mistakes remain the sole responsibility of the authors. As they have worked independently, the views and analysis expressed in this document remain those of the authors and do not necessarily represent the views of the supporters, trustees, or other staff at the Fraser Institute.

Publishing information

Distribution   These publications are available from <http://www.fraserinstitute.org> in Portable Document Format (PDF) and can be read with Adobe Acrobat® or Adobe Reader®, versions 7 or later. Adobe Reader® XI, the most recent version, is available free of charge from Adobe Systems Inc. at <http://get.adobe.com/reader/>. Readers having trouble viewing or printing our PDF files using applications from other manufacturers (e.g., Apple's Preview) should use Reader® or Acrobat®.

Ordering publications   To order printed publications from the Fraser Institute, please contact the publications coordinator:
- e-mail: sales@fraserinstitute.org
- telephone: 604.688.0221 ext. 580 or, toll free, 1.800.665.3558 ext. 580
- fax: 604.688.8539

Media   For media enquiries, please contact our Communications Department:
- 604.714.4582
- e-mail: communications@fraserinstitute.org.

Date of issue   2014
ISBN   978-0-88975-304-4
Printed and bound in Canada

Citation   Murphy, Robert P., Jason Clemens, Milagros Palacios, and Niels Veldhuis (2014). *Economic Principles for Prosperity*. Fraser Institute.

Cover design and artwork   Monica Thomas, Foothills Graphics

Cover images   Stephen Avenue Walk in Calgary, Canada © Ronniechua, Dreamstime.com

Supporting the Fraser Institute

To learn how to support the Fraser Institute, please contact

- Development Department, Fraser Institute
  Fourth Floor, 1770 Burrard Street
  Vancouver, British Columbia, V6J 3G7 Canada
- telephone, toll-free: 1.800.665.3558 ext. 586
- e-mail: development@fraserinstitute.org

Purpose, funding, & independence

The Fraser Institute provides a useful public service. We report objective information about the economic and social effects of current public policies, and we offer evidence-based research and education about policy options that can improve the quality of life.

The Institute is a non-profit organization. Our activities are funded by charitable donations, unrestricted grants, ticket sales, and sponsorships from events, the licensing of products for public distribution, and the sale of publications.

All research is subject to rigorous review by external experts, and is conducted and published separately from the Institute's Board of Trustees and its donors.

The opinions expressed by the authors are those of the individuals themselves, and do not necessarily reflect those of the Institute, its Board of Trustees, its donors and supporters, or its staff. This publication in no way implies that the Fraser Institute, its trustees, or staff are in favour of, or oppose the passage of, any bill; or that they support or oppose any particular political party or candidate.

As a healthy part of public discussion among fellow citizens who desire to improve the lives of people through better public policy, the Institute welcomes evidence-focused scrutiny of the research we publish, including verification of data sources, replication of analytical methods, and intelligent debate about the practical effects of policy recommendations.

About the Fraser Institute

Our vision is a free and prosperous world where individuals benefit from greater choice, competitive markets, and personal responsibility. Our mission is to measure, study, and communicate the impact of competitive markets and government interventions on the welfare of individuals.

Founded in 1974, we are an independent Canadian research and educational organization with locations throughout North America and international partners in over 85 countries. Our work is financed by tax-deductible contributions from thousands of individuals, organizations, and foundations. In order to protect its independence, the Institute does not accept grants from government or contracts for research.

Nous envisageons un monde libre et prospère, où chaque personne bénéficie d'un plus grand choix, de marchés concurrentiels et de responsabilités individuelles. Notre mission consiste à mesurer, à étudier et à communiquer l'effet des marchés concurrentiels et des interventions gouvernementales sur le bien-être des individus.

Peer review—validating the accuracy of our research

The Fraser Institute maintains a rigorous peer review process for its research. New research, major research projects, and substantively modified research conducted by the Fraser Institute are reviewed by experts with a recognized expertise in the topic area being addressed. Whenever possible, external review is a blind process. Updates to previously reviewed research or new editions of previously reviewed research are not reviewed unless the update includes substantive or material changes in the methodology.

The review process is overseen by the directors of the Institute's research departments who are responsible for ensuring all research published by the Institute passes through the appropriate peer review. If a dispute about the recommendations of the reviewers should arise during the Institute's peer review process, the Institute has an Editorial Advisory Board, a panel of scholars from Canada, the United States, and Europe to whom it can turn for help in resolving the dispute.

Editorial Advisory Board